A colour guide to familiar
FRESHWATER
FISHES

By Dr Jiří Čihař

Illustrated by Jiří Malý

Translated by Daniela Coxon
Graphic design: Soňa Valoušková

This paperback edition first published 1983 by
OCTOPUS BOOKS LIMITED
59, Grosvenor Street, London, W 1

Reprinted 1984, 1986

ISBN 0 7064 1971 5

Printed in Czechoslovakia by Svoboda
3/10/12/51-07

CONTENTS

Foreword   7

Freshwater as a Living Space   9

Fish — Primitive yet Fascinating   15

Spawning   20

Parental Care   25

Breeding Migrations of the Salmon and the Eel   29

Early Life of a Fish   33

How and What Fishes Eat   37

Fish and Man   41

Fish Food   44

Plates   47-175

Industrial Fishing   176

Bibliography   180

Index of Common Names   181

Index of Latin Names   183

FOREWORD

Skin diving with watertight goggles, flippers and a snorkel or an aqualung every year attracts a greater number of people and has gradually become one of the most popular sports. Its ever-increasing popularity is not surprising as skin diving gives man an opportunity to get to know the unknown world of the seas, which for centuries has kept its secrets and left man literally in the dark. The surface of seas and freshwaters screens a magnificent world of incredibly varied colours and shapes. Shallow coastal seas heated by the sun and enhanced by coral cliffs naturally attract man's attention because of their abundance of colourful fish and splendid variety of other incredible sea animals. However, a similar interest is also warranted by the waters of rivers and streams, pools, ponds and lakes, which up to now have been by many people unjustly neglected.

The purpose of this book is to introduce to the reader the best known and economically most important fishes of such freshwaters. They are described just as they were seen during the author's diving expeditions; often this involved very close observation, which facilitated an accurate appreciation of their beautiful colouring and graceful movement and also the penetration of their secluded existence. It is in fact possible to get very close to fish, providing that the observer remains motionless and does not disturb them by sudden movements.

When a fish is caught and pulled out of the water, even the most colourful specimen loses its iridescent colours in a matter of minutes. It becomes only a pale image of the colourful and active creature, which only a few moments before was so fascinating underwater. In order to present fish in their natural habitat, a fresh attempt at collaboration has been tried between the ichthyologist, that is the zoologist who studies fishes and their life cycle, and the illustrator, whose task it is to reproduce faithfully the transient beauty of fish and their characteristic movements. The illustrations of fish produced in this book have resulted from such direct observation; they are represented the way in which the artist recorded and recalled them in his colour sketches.

The life of fishes below the water surface and their movement in aquaria has been a subject of study for several years and has produced a collection of photographs, drawings and colour sketches, which have been used in the compilation of this book. These are prefaced by several brief chapters which discuss some interesting facts about the life of European freshwater fishes and relate experiences in catching fish in nets and hooks. Pictures of live fish follow and are accompanied by descriptions of the individual species with brief data about their distribution and way of life.

It is hoped that this book will generally arouse interest in the mysterious underwater life to be found in both running and still waters. The world about us is still full of secrets and puzzles and such detailed observation of fishes and other aquatic creatures cannot but reveal a number of interesting features and surprises.

FRESHWATER AS A LIVING SPACE

Running and still waters provide every landscape with a definite character. Wells, streams and torrents, lowland rivers, old waterways, lakes, reservoirs and ponds create a specific habitat for many plants and animals. Such waters are inhabited by distinctive plant and animal kingdoms, in which every member has a strictly defined role. Green water plants assimilate and build up new living tissues and at the same time maintain a balance between the amount of carbon dioxide and oxygen in the water. They are the main source of food for a large group of animals, who transform such vegetation into animal matter, which in turn becomes the food of other animals. In contrast another group of aquatic organisms lives on dead plants and animals' bodies and similarly recycles existing nutriments.

Life in the water is fundamentally different from that in the air. Primarily the density of water is many times higher; therefore when water creatures move, they have to overcome a much greater resistance than that experienced by dry land animals. At the same time their density is usually roughly equal to that of water and this makes them buoyant and enables them to move with little effort in their water environment.

Like air, water must satisfy the basic requirements of an animal in order to sustain and successfully develop life. It must have a suitable temperature, adequate oxygen content, and provide other inorganic and organic substances. Although the temperature of the air fluctuates much more than the temperature of water, the amount of oxygen in the air, whatever the temperature, is always the same. On the other hand, the amount of oxygen in the water rapidly decreases with any rise in temperature.

In the course of respiration, fish and other water animals use up the oxygen in the water and replace it with carbon dioxide, which is then transformed by green water plants through the process of photosynthesis into vegetable protein and fats. The plants again release oxygen into the water. However, photosynthesis only takes place in daylight, as at night the same green plants absorb oxygen from the water and breathe out carbon dioxide. In running water the oxygen content is substantially restored direct from the air, but in still waters green algae and other water plants sometimes spread profusely and at night produce a drop in the oxygen level. This can lead to the death of fish and other more sensitive animals living in such waters. However, different species of fish do not need the same amount of oxygen. Some species, such as the trout and the bullhead, require more oxygen than the majority of fish belonging to the carp family. Therefore the trout and the bullhead are most abundant only in the cold and well oxygenated water of mountain streams and rivers, while carp, bream, roach and other members of the carp family prefer warm, sunlit lowland waters. The optimal water temperature for the brown trout is between 12° to 15° C and for carp between 22° to 25° C. If the water temperature rises for any length of time, the fish will die. Some European fish, such as the weatherfish, can continue to breathe, however, even in unfavourable conditions.

The weatherfish lives in overgrown, muddy ditches which link together ponds, also in pools and oxbow lakes. If the water is short of oxygen, the fish rise to the water surface and swallow air, and so absorb oxygen through their intestinal membranes, which are well supplied with blood.

In extremely poor conditions the crucian carp can even itself produce the oxygen necessary for its existence. This unusual ability deserves a closer investigation. Densely overgrown pools and oxbow lakes can in fact be abundantly populated with its dwarf variety, which only occasionally reaches a length of 10 cm. As opposed to the other, ordinary crucian carp, it has a stunted and relatively long body. It grows very slowly and barely achieves a length of 10 cm even after eight or nine years. However, the way this fish lives in unfavourable conditions for several years without suffering any damage is remarkable. The greater part of the year it lives in water which completely lacks oxygen, although on the other hand such water contains a high percentage of carbon dioxide and hydrogen sulphide. Any other fish would soon start to suffocate and die in such a habitat, but these small crucian carp can live in such conditions as a result of their unusual ability to produce the oxygen necessary for their existence by breaking down their body fat. This ability is called anaerobic metabolism and is generally a characteristic of some invertebrates — intestinal parasites such as tapeworm and flatworm — while in vertebrates it is unique.

The stunted crucian carp can even survive when frozen for a short time along with plants in the ice. This feature is a characteristic of the North American and Siberian fish *Dallia pectoralis*, which is a relative of the pike. It revives even after a lengthy frozen period, providing that its body tissues have remained unaffected. However, if the body cells freeze, that is if the water in its body crystallizes, then the fish dies.

The temperature of the water also plays an important part in the reproduction of fish, in fact it is one of its basic preconditions. It also determines the length of time that fish embryos take to develop from the egg. Trout, a well-known hardy species, spawn in the icy water of mountain streams during the winter months, whereas members of the carp family require considerably warmer water. For example, the carp will only spawn, when the water temperature rises above 16 °C.

The influence of the water temperature is very important in terms of the provision of fish food. It is noticeable that the increase in the fish population is much smaller in cold years than in warm ones. Most freshwater fishes feed on minute or small water animals. In the fast-flowing waters of streams and rivers, these take the form of small animals living on the river bed, whilst in still waters such food is supplemented by plankton.

Plankton consists of minute animals and plants which float in the water and the majority of species are characterized by their own inconspicuous yet active movements. These organisms include such typical microscopic structures as single-celled algae, protozoa and minute rotifers as well as small crustaceans. The most common of these are cyclops and daphnia, which are known to every aquarist. Planktonic plant life is

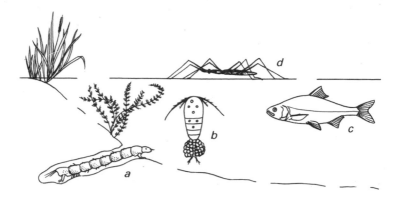

Fig. 1. Types of water communities: a) benthos, b) plankton, c) nekton, d) pleuston.

called phytoplankton and animal plankton is known as zooplankton.

Another group of organisms, called nekton, consists of animals which besides floating are also capable of swimming. Nekton includes the larvae of aquatic insects, beetles and especially fish. The minute organisms which live in the surface water layers are called neuston and they chiefly consist of protozoa, such as flagellates. Animals which use the water surface as a basis for movement are called pleuston. The most common animals belonging to this group are the slender, long-legged water boatman, black water beetles and also various types of daphnia, which swim suspended from the water surface.

Organisms that live on the water bottom are called benthos and they represent the most important food component for fish living in fast-flowing waters. They include the larvae of various water insects, such as the mayfly, stonefly, caddis fly and red midge; crustaceans, such as freshwater shrimp; some molluscs and worms. An important source of food for the trout, grayling, chub and other fish are insects which fall onto the water surface. Finally, large specimens of some fish species become predators and eat smaller fish, including their own species.

Specific types of freshwater habitats are populated by different groups of animals, which together form unique animal communities. A characteristic animal community inhabits, for example, the fast-flowing waters of mountain streams and waterfalls. Such a habitat offers cold and clear water, rich in oxygen. Animals living in such a habitat are often equipped with various types of suction discs, located on the abdomen, which prevent them from being carried away by a strong water current. Their body shape is also adapted to such strong currents, as they are usually flattened, which enables them to cling to any type of water bed. The most frequently represented group in such an environment are invertebrates, like the larvae of the mayfly, stonefly and caddis fly. Similarly the typical fish of this sort of habitat is the brown trout, which gives its name to the trout zone, as this area of fast-flowing mountain waters and waterfalls is called. Of course, there also live in these waters other fish species; still pools under rocks are the hideouts of the small, large-headed bullhead, whilst deep and quiet pools are inhabited by the colourful and lively minnow, the long-barbelled horned pout, the chub and the small lamprey.

Different species live in mountain streams and lowland rivers, where the water level is deeper, its descent is more gradual and the water temperature is somewhat higher. However, the trout and some other fishes of the upper reaches can also be seen in these parts. A typical fish of such submountainous waters with their sandy or gravelly bottoms is the grayling and therefore this part of the river is often called the grayling zone. There are also other fish that live here, such as the gudgeon, the barbel, and in the Danube system the huchen and the nase. However, not all rivers have a distinct grayling zone.

A typical fish of larger, deeper, fast-flowing rivers below the mountain zone is the barbel and hence this section of the river is often called the barbel zone. Other fish commonly found here are the chub, the pike, the burbot, the dace, sometimes the perch and even the carp.

Lowland, slow-flowing, deep waters with numerous oxbow

lakes and pools provide the home for many species of the carp family, such as the bream, the silver bream, the roach, the carp, the rudd, the asp, the zahrte and the bleak. Also the pike, the wels, the zander, the perch and the eel can be frequently found in this area. Once again, because the most common and most characteristic fish of such still lowland rivers is the bream, this zone has been named after it.

Closely related communities of fish and other aquatic animals are to be found in the large lowland reservoirs and lakes. Unfortunately the living conditions of such areas are often adversely influenced by the frequent and often extreme fluctuations in the water level, which at times make it impossible for fish to breed successfully. In this area, as well as in oxbow lakes and pools, plankton constitutes an important component of fish food. However, the largest amount of plankton is present in ponds and artificial reservoirs which are regularly purified, enriched with calcium and periodically relieved of undesirable water vegetation, whilst economically important fish, such as the carp, pike, tench and the zander are stocked in them. Such ponds and reservoirs are usually drained from time to time and the fish are caught.

An entirely distinctive biotope is created by the glacial mountain lakes to be found in the Alps, in Scandinavia, Ireland and Scotland. These are populated by various species and varieties of the charr, the whitefish, the brown and lake trout and also by quite unique, indigenous fish species.

FISH — PRIMITIVE YET FASCINATING

Cyclostomes and fishes belong to the oldest known vertebrates on our planet, as their ancestors lived some four to five hundred million years ago, in the early Silurian period. They constitute the first link in the developmental chain of vertebrates but unlike other vertebrates remained associated with their water habitat for millions of years. At a much later date, the first aquatic animals crept to dry land and became the original predecessors of today's land vertebrates, such as amphibians, reptiles, birds and mammals.

While probably fewer than 100 Cyclostome species have survived in the sea and freshwater, the number of fishes is very high indeed, roughly 20,000 to 25,000 species, constituting about a half of the total number of living vertebrates. They can be found in all types of aquatic habitats, ranging from the deepest seas to the mountain lakes at around 5,000 metres above sea level; from the tributaries of the South American Lake Titicaca, to the freezing waters of the Antarctic or in sharply contrasting tropical rivers and pools, whilst some fish species even live in hot springs. Of the total number of fish species in the world, only a small proportion are to be found in European freshwaters.

The most primitive vertebrates are the Cyclostomes. They include the marine hag-fishes and lampreys found in both the sea and freshwater. They have an elongated, worm-like body, a cartilaginous skeleton and the paired fins are missing. Their skin is smooth and scaleless and so at first sight they do not look like vertebrates. Lampreys have a round, suctorial, funnel-like mouth, covered with sharp, horny teeth. The centre of the funnel contains a toothed tongue, which functions like a piston. It is an effective sucking device, by means of which lampreys suck the body juices and grind the muscles of fish and invertebrates.

Fig. 2. Types of fish mouth: a) terminal mouth, b) inferior or ventral mouth, c) oblique or dorsal mouth.

The class of true fishes (Teleostei) differs from the more primitive Cyclostome vertebrates and the elasmobranchs, such as the shark, ray and the strange chimera, by having a firm, bony skeleton. Fishes as opposed to the jawless lamprey have a well-developed skull and jaws. The majority have a scale-covered body, but there are also many scaleless fish. One of these is a giant amongst European fish, namely the wels. On the other hand the bodies of other fishes, such as the large sturgeon, are covered with longitudinal rows of large, bony shields.

The movement of fish is made possible by their fins. The majority have a pair of pectoral and pelvic fins, a single dorsal, caudal and anal fin. However, some fish do not have pelvic or pectoral fins, whilst others lack the dorsal or the caudal fin. The eel is one such example as it has no pelvic fins, whilst its dorsal, caudal and anal fins are fused together to form a continuous fin edging.

The body shape of fishes is also subject to great variations. The most usual is the streamlined body, typical of the trout, roach, zander or carp. However, another form is the elongated, serpent-like body, such as that of the eel. In contrast the flounder has a very flat body, asymmetrical in mature specimens. Thus, they are an exception amongst vertebrates. Most other fish and a majority of all the animals in the world are perfectly symmetrical, which means that the left side of their body is in fact a mirror reflection of the right side.

However, the external body features of fish are insufficient to classify them, and must be supplemented by further anatomical features. Basically the structure of every fish body is the same, with the exception of the spine, which in the more primitive, less developed fish is cartilaginous, whilst in more advanced species it is made of bone.

As regards size, European freshwater fishes contain specimens which are very large as well as very small. The largest freshwater fish is a sturgeon, the beluga, a true giant, which lives in the rivers flowing into the Black Sea. The largest specimen caught measured some nine metres and weighed about one and a half tons. In contrast, the common sturgeon, which is a relative of the beluga, rarely grows to a length of three and a half metres and weighs about 300 kg. The wels is also one of the largest fish found in rivers and reservoirs, although nowadays large specimens measuring three metres and weighing about 100 kg are exceptional. However, in the past wels specimens living in the River Danube and its tributaries, were much larger. For example, in 1726 one was caught, which weighed

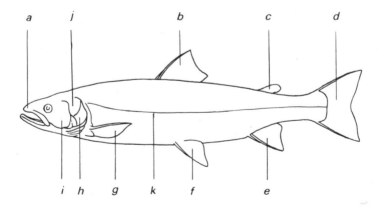

Fig. 3. Body of a member of the salmon family: a) snout, b) dorsal fin, c) adipose fin, d) caudal fin, e) anal fin, f) pelvic fins, g) pectoral fins, h) sub-opercle bone, i) pre-opercle, j) opercle, k) lateral line.

17

340 kg. Record specimens of the pike grow to a length of one and a half metres and weigh 35 to 40 kg, whilst the large salmon and huchen can reach a similar length and an even greater weight in excess of 50 kg. Other fish, such as the sea and lake trout, zander, barbel and carp can also achieve large sizes. On several occasions in fact carp have been caught, measuring more than one metre and weighing over 30 kg.

The smallest European fish include the moderlieschen and bitterling, which usually measure only five to six centimetres, whilst the spined loach is a little longer, but more slender. Nevertheless, even such small European species are still gigantic when compared with the dwarf fish of the tropical zones. The smallest fish in the world, called *Pandaka pygmaea*, which comes from the Philippines, measures only seven to ten millimetres in the adult stage and the proportionately minute size of its fry can well be imagined.

The question of the age to which fish usually live is an interesting one. Many fish species, including some members of the carp family, such as the moderlieschen, minnow or gudgeon, live only one or a few years. On the other hand, large carp, pike, catfish, trout or barbel can live for several tens of years. However, exaggerated stories of carp living for several centuries definitely belong to the world of legends and fairy tales. The greatest age recorded for such giant fish from the sturgeon family as the huge beluga or common sturgeon, is a little over a hundred years.

Today the age of a fish can be determined with a relative degree of accuracy by the structure of the fish's scales and some bones (e.g. the vertebrae or the bones of the gill cover). The course of the fish's growth in the preceding years can similarly be traced as the annual growth rate is clearly indicated on the scales and such bones. For example the perimeter of the scales hardly increases during the period when the fish do not feed or accept only a limited food supply. Such periods are characterized by a dark, non-transparent strip on the scale.

On the other hand, in summer, when fish are feeding intensively and growing fast, the perimeter measurement of their scales rapidly expands. Summer growth is therefore readily

Fig. 4. Types of fish scales: a) cycloid scale of the carp species.   b) ctenoid scale of the perch species,   c) 1, 2, 3, 4 — annual growth rings.

identifiable by the addition of wide, lighter circles to the scale edges. The dark winter circles of the fish scales can also be easily counted with the help of a magnifying glass or a microscope and in this way the number of winters through which a fish has lived is easily determined. Finally, the distance between the individual winter growth rings and the centre of the scale reflects the rate of fish growth in the preceding years. A concluding thought is that in contrast to warm-blooded vertebrates, fish may grow continuously throughout their entire existence and thus their growth has no terminal point as long as they live.

SPAWNING

The spawning period is the annual climax in the life of fish and provides a most interesting sight for the casual observer. In this introduction some basic information about fish reproduction must therefore be considered.

None of the European species is viviparous, i.e. the spawn is fertilized in the female body. All fish in European freshwaters spawn directly into the water. According to the spawning habitat and the substrate onto which the spawn is deposited, fish can be divided into several groups. The largest group is formed by the species which spawn in aquatic vegetation or flooded meadows and whose spawn adheres to such aquatic plants. They include the majority of the carp family, such as the carp, the common bream, usually the roach and the rudd and also the weatherfish, the carnivorous pike and a number of other fish. A similar type of spawning is made on the bare roots of water plants and on the lesser roots of undermined trees or on submerged branches, coniferous needles, etc.

A further group is formed by fish which spawn on submerged stones or a gravelly base. They include the asp, nase, orfe, chub, zahrte, barbel, sturgeon and many others. This group also includes those species which attach their spawn to stones, gravel or sand and then bury them so that they are not carried away by a strong current or endangered by predators.

Other fish, for example the ziege, which is the only representative of this group to be found in European freshwaters, have pelagic spawn, which are freely deposited into the water, where they float and are subsequently carried away by the current. A very unusual and danger-free location is chosen for its new generation by the bitterling, the smallest European fish. With the help of an ovipositor the female lays a relatively small quantity of spawn directly into the mantle cavity of the swan mussel. A more protected cradle is difficult to imagine.

Some fish species which lay a large number of eggs, such as the carp, the pike, the tench or the burbot, do not look after their offspring. The reason for this is that the tiny fish hatch from only a small percentage of the deposited spawn and hence only a few grow and reach maturity, but nevertheless it is still highly probable that from such a large number of eggs there will be some survivors. On the other hand, those species which produce only a small number of eggs, such as the mud minnow, the bitterling, the salmon and the grayling, must ensure the safety of their offspring. Therefore, they reproduce in a variety of hideouts or alternatively bury their spawn in the gravel and others construct a nest over which one or both parents stand guard.

The majority of fish live constantly in the places where they also spawn. However, some species travel a long distance to reach a suitable mating ground. These include the eel, the salmon, the sea trout, some herring and some members of the carp family, such as the nase and zahrte.

The spawning process of fish is a most interesting phenomenon to observe. The majority of European fish spawn when the water is pleasantly warm for man; it is however often unnecessary to be in the water to watch the spawning procedure, as fish can be easily observed in shallow waters from a small boat with a glass bottom. Fish are not shy during the breeding season and consequently are neither frightened by the boat nor by man himself should he mingle with them.

The first stage to be observed is the preparatory courtship period, during which the males chase the females, bite their belly and head and rub against their sides and back. This is followed by the males swimming with unusual jerky movements amongst the water plants, alternately opening their fins wide apart, then pressing them close to their bodies and finally shaking in sequence their dorsal and pectoral fins. Their movements in this phase of spawning are reminiscent of birds floating in the air. Whilst the male parades himself, the female either lies motionless or slowly follows him around. The culmination of this ceremony takes place when individual pairs swim together in the shallows close to the water surface, press against each other's sides and whilst both bodies move in spasmodic jerks with their caudal fins flapping, the females shed their spawn and the males milt. Spawn in clouds of white milt then disperses into the immediate vicinity and sticks to adjacent aquatic vegetation. The climax is a very short one, lasting only a few seconds. Then the fish part for some time to rest on the water bed only to resume the same process later, often with another partner.

Many fish species do not shed all their spawn at once, because this only ripens gradually and therefore the whole ceremony is repeated in two or three weeks. However, the second milting is usually not as stormy a process as the first, and not as many pairs are involved. The quantity of ejected spawn is not as great, although it is still very important. Often after the initial spawning the water level in the river or lake drops and the spawn are left on dry land. At other times there is a sudden, sharp drop in temperature, which similarly kills the fish embryos. The second spawning therefore ensures that the species survives in such eventualities.

An unusual mating ritual is that performed by the salmon and the grayling. Adult grayling migrate in spring from the lower to the upper reaches of rivers, battling against the seasonal strong currents. On arrival every male occupies a specific area, which is usually separated from the territory of another male by large stones, sandy shallows, uprooted trees or other obstacles. Such territory is then jealously protected from other fish, both male and female. Sometimes grayling males have bitter fights with one another, during which they provoke and bite each other until the stronger opponent triumphs and the weaker is chased away.

After this defence of his spawning area, the male hovers about its centre and slowly spreads out his beautifully coloured fins until his whole body vibrates. At the same time he advances towards one or several females, which are waiting some distance away. If the female is ready to spawn, she draws near to the male and invites him to join in the mating ceremony by adopting a special pose. She bends her back and draws in her dorsal fin close to the body. The male then presses close to her, covers

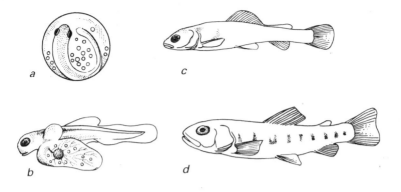

5. Development of a salmon: a) egg,   b) alevin,   c) fry,   d) parr.

her with his high dorsal fin and both fish swim in slow jerky movements to the centre of the territory. Suddenly both fish start to vibrate, the female arches her back and presses her belly into the gravel to lay her eggs, which are then fertilized by the male. At this moment both fish open heir mouths wide, whilst the spawn is becoming firmly attached to the gravel. The spawning process itself lasts only several seconds and after the ceremony the male chases the female away, who nevertheless returns after a while and the whole procedure is repeated. Immediately after the final spawning the female leaves the spawning grounds.

The trout's mating ceremony is again different; the spawning ground is in fact prepared by the female, who digs shallow, bowl-like hollows in the water bed with sharp strokes of her body, while the male stands facing the current behind her. Only when the spawning ground is thus prepared does the male join the female, who then arches her body and in spasmodic bursts sheds her golden yellow spawn. This particular spawning process lasts a relatively long time. The female repeatedly comes back to the spawning ground accompanied by the persistent male, whilst her movements during spawning are so strong that the sand and small stones swirl around and cover the spawn.

No less interesting is the spawning of small freshwater lampreys, for even these primitive vertebrates construct a spawning nest. The major responsibility rests on the female, who attaches herself to small stones and loosens them so that they are carried away by the water current and thus the area is made ready for spawning. During spawning the male fastens himself to the female behind her and twists his body around her. The female then sheds her eggs, which are fertilized by the male. After spawning, the male is carried away by the water current, leaving the female attached to a stone and burying the fertilized spawn with quick undulating movements of her body. After this process the adult lampreys die.

PARENTAL CARE

In the majority of fish, parental care ends immediately after spawning. The female lays the eggs, the male fertilizes them with his milt and the future generation is left to its own devices. However, some fish do take better care of their offspring.

In many fish species parental care is the exact reverse of human practice, as the female role ends with the laying of the spawn, whilst the male looks after the fertilized spawn and the hatched embryos. In the group of freshwater fishes the wels stands out as the most devoted of parents. When the female spawns into the carefully constructed nest close to the river bank, the male then fertilizes the spawn and looks after them by himself. He continues to stay close to the nest and chases away other fish which would like to get hold of such an attractive delicacy. The horned pout, its distant North American relative, which was introduced to European waters at the end of the last and the beginning of this century and which has multiplied considerably in suitable habitats, gives similar care and devotion to its spawn.

In addition, the males of another two North American species, the large-mouth bass and the pumpkinseed, which have similarly adapted themselves to European habitats, look after their spawn most diligently. The large-mouth bass male builds bowl-shaped nests with a diameter of about 60 to 80 cm on the bottom at a depth of up to two metres. Here he guards the fertilized spawn. Similar nests 20 to 30 cm in diameter are built on the bottom by the male pumpkinseed. Initially he chooses a location and then carefully clears the ground of the fine muddy silt with his mouth to reveal the rough gravelly base. He goes on removing stones to make a shallow hollow. Finally, the male hangs motionless above the nest, slowly begins to tremble and then swims jerkily towards the females, who in turn approach the nest. He selects one of them and then both fish swim side by side above the centre of the nest, where the female lays her eggs and the male fertilizes them. Afterwards the male vigilantly guards the nest hovering above it and fiercely chases away all enemies and intruders. Because individual nests in a large colony are usually close together, the patrolling males regularly fight each other, attacking their rivals and trying to chase them away with their dorsal, anal and caudal fins spread wide apart.

During experiments, a colony guarded by such pumpkinseed males was closely observed. An arm outstretched towards a nest was immediately attacked by the fearless father and although the fish was quite small, measuring only 10 to 15 cm, it was obviously not afraid of anything.

The zander builds large nests about 50 cm in diameter in shallow waters close to river banks. They excavate a hollow several centimetres deep and loosen the roots of water vegetation, especially those of reeds. Then the female attaches to them a large quantity of spawn, which can embody anything up to a million eggs. Having fertilized the spawn, the male carefully guards the nest, driving in fresh oxygenated water with a continuous movement of his fins and at the same time clearing away any layers of fine mud. During these paternal duties the male zander does not receive any food.

Small moderlieschen, which fasten their spawn to aquatic vegetation, also assiduously guard their offspring, whilst the large-headed bullhead and the Alpine bullhead of the trout zone are similarly fussy parents. In each case the spawn is guarded by the male, after the female has attached it to the underside of a stone resting freely on the water bed, so that there is a ready-made hollow for it. During the incubation period, when embryos are developing in the spawn, the male stays close to his stone and chases away all enemies who threaten to endanger the spawn.

Also stickleback males make good, attentive parents. Some species even build regular ball-shaped nests with two circular entrances. Others, for example the three-spined stickleback *(Gasterosteus aculeatus)* build less tidy nests from water plants and roots. Male sticklebacks guard not only the spawn, but also the young fry, that is until the yolk sac of the embryo becomes fully absorbed and the fish leave the nest.

A very interesting reproductive process is that of the smallest European fish, the bitterling. In the breeding season the males are beautifully coloured, their sides glisten with a violet-blue sheen and they have two black patches behind the head and a blue-green fluorescent stripe which widens out along the back. Their dorsal and anal fins are flaming red and edged in black, whilst the body of the females even during spawning remains a shimmering silver colour. Behind the anal opening a long pink ovipositor develops, which is inserted into the valves of mussels so deep that it ultimately penetrates the mantle cavity. There they lay one or two large eggs, which adhere to the gills of the mussel. The male then sheds its milt directly above the inhalant siphon of the mussel and this is drawn in along with a fresh water current and thus the spawn is fertilized. Several bitterling regularly spawn into one mussel, so that at any point in time its mantle cavity contains a number of bitterling at various stages of development. The bitterling embryos develop inside the mussel until they hatch, when they leave the mussel through its respiratory aperture and swim into free water.

The mussel larvae, called glochidia, 'revenge' themselves for their parents being thus exploited by the bitterling spawn. They in turn attach themselves by means of small hooks to the skin, fins or gills of the bitterling or other fish species and live as parasites on their bodies for two to three weeks. Then they detach themselves and live independently. In this way the fish ensure the spread of mussels throughout rivers and ponds. In all the above-mentioned fish it is the father who looks after the spawn and small fry, but in the case of the mud minnow *(Umbra krameri)* it is the mother who takes care of her offspring. The mud minnow is a small fish which lives in the watershed of the River Danube, especially in shallow waters which have become densely overgrown with water vegetation. It spawns in April in a temperature of 12° to 18 °C. The females build special nests for their eggs on the bottom and these are miniature copies of the nests built by the large-mouth bass, the pumpkinseed or the zander. The females do not build these nests with their mouth, but with their fins and belly. They remove all the mud until they reach the clean sand, but sometimes they only remove that around the roots of water vegetation. This activity takes a long time, sometimes as much as several days. When the female builds the nest, she is in a very aggressive mood and chases away much larger fish than herself. When she is finally satisfied with her creation, she hovers above it and fans it with her fins. When she is ready to spawn her aggressiveness recedes for a time. A single male then approaches the female, presses himself close to her above the nest and after a while both fish begin to shiver and spawn.

After milting the male loses his deep colouring, whereas the female becomes even more intensively coloured and once again very aggressive. She jealously guards her spawn, swims constantly above the nest and fans it with fast movements of her pectoral fins to stop it being covered with mud. She usually guards the nest in this manner for about ten days, when the young fry hatch out.

BREEDING MIGRATIONS
OF THE SALMON AND THE EEL

If a fish species makes a particular journey in large shoals at a specific time in the year it is called migration, which has parallels in the migrating habits of birds.

This migration of fish can be caused by any of three reasons. Firstly, it is simply a matter of travelling in search of food, as in the case of the herring, pilchard, mackerel, cod, tuna and other sea species; secondly, such journeys can be made for the purpose of mating, as in the case of the salmon, eel, some whitefishes and lampreys; or finally, it can be a migration journey whose objective is to find the most suitable place for hibernation. This type of migration is common in many fish of the carp family; these migrate in late autumn to the lower reaches of rivers, where, often at great depths, they live through the hard winter season. The fish which migrate from seas in order to mate in freshwaters are called anadromous. Examples are the sea lamprey and the salmon. In contrast catadromous fish, such as the eel, travel from freshwaters to spawn in the sea. As these 'mysterious' migrations have for centuries constituted the greatest zoological puzzle for man, they are worth discussing.

A classic example is the salmon *(Salmo salar)*, which lives in the Atlantic ocean basin. However, during the spawning period it embarks on long journeys from the sea to river estuaries and finally swims upriver against the current to the place where it was born several years before. During this journey the adult male salmon develops a kype, that is a hook on the lower jaw. It does not eat and has to battle against rapids, surmount waterfalls and weirs. Once in the upper reaches of rivers, where the current is still very strong, it digs deep hollows about two metres long in the sandy or gravelly river bed, where the females lay their eggs which, after the males have fertilized them, are covered by sand and gravel. After spawning most salmon die through sheer exhaustion, but some of them make the return journey to the sea and the following year they repeat their mating migration all over again. The salmon embryos, which hatch from the spawn, stay in these freshwaters usually for two or three years; then they gradually drift with the current of the river towards the sea.

Whilst in freshwater the young salmon feed on various invertebrates, as opposed to the sea where their diet consists mainly of fish. After two or three years in the sea, they will have grown a great deal and will have stored in their muscles large amounts of fat, which contains substances that change the basic colour of the salmon to red. When adult, they begin to migrate from the sea and upriver to the spawning grounds.

At the end of the last and at the beginning of this century salmon were still very abundant in the majority of European rivers, such as the Elbe, Rhine and Weser. However, nowadays large European rivers usually prove to be inaccessible for salmon; high weirs, sluices, dams and water pollution have put an end to mating migration by stopping them from reaching their spawning grounds. However, salmon are still numerous in northern Norwegian and Swedish rivers, in those rivers flowing into the Baltic sea, in Scotland, Ireland and Iceland and along the western shores of Greenland.

It is only in recent years that the mystery of salmon migration journeys has been adequately explained, particularly such questions as to why they always rediscover their native river and what regulates their journey so that they never make a mistake and enter another river to spawn. For it has been proved by marking fish that they only spawn in the place of their birth.

Salmon have a well-developed ability to recognize by taste and smell the quality of the water. Their native river has for them a quite typical and distinctive taste and smell. The chemical composition of the water therefore guides them not only during their long journey upriver, but also during their journey across the sea. Salmon specimens whose organs of smell and taste were neutralized so that they were unable to taste or smell the river of their birth wandered helplessly along the sea shore and in the end swam into any river to spawn. On the other hand, normal salmon found their native birth place very quickly and without hesitation. In other experiments salmon embryos have been placed in ponds with water containing chemical additives and in the spawning season it then proved possible to entice the salmon by means of these chemicals from the sea into any river. Similar migratory journeys from seas to freshwaters are undertaken every year by the migrating species of the lamprey (e.g. sea lamprey), which are to be found swimming upriver during the spring months of March and April. When the lampreys have to overcome strong currents, weirs or waterfalls during a particularly tiresome journey, they often attach themselves to stones and have a rest. They also often travel upriver attached to other migrating fishes, such as the sea trout or the salmon, and sometimes are even found fastened to a ship's keel. Sea lamprey spawn in small groups in the upper river reaches in May, June and July. Their larvae, called prides, live in freshwaters for about four years and then for a substantially longer period in the sea, where they feed parasitically on a number of sea fish. Adult lampreys, whose digestive organs often degenerate during their journey upriver, do not eat in this period and die after spawning.

Another well-known migratory fish which travels, however, from freshwater to spawn in the sea, is the eel. Although the biology of the eel in freshwaters had been studied in some detail by the end of the nineteenth century, no systematic explanation had been achieved of the eel's migratory or mating habits. It was always known that the large shoals of adult eel migrated every autumn downriver into the sea, but no one had detected the adult fish returning again from the sea to freshwater. But every spring millions of small young eel, seven to ten centimetres long and called elvers, regularly appeared off the European and North American coasts in the river estuaries. Their numbers were so great that catching them was a minor industry. Even today, large quantities of elvers are still transplanted every year into European inland rivers and ponds.

The eel's birthplace, however, still remained unknown and

therefore in 1905 a systematic study of the life cycle of the eel began. A team of scientists led by Dr. Schmidt, a Danish biologist and oceanographer, worked assiduously on board ship at sea and discovered that the earliest stages of the eel, the tiny *Leptocephalus*, inhabited the remoter parts of the Atlantic Ocean, in the vicinity of the Sargasso Sea, which lies south-east of the Bermudas. It is a large area in which the long, tough sea algae *(Sargassum)* abounds, and constitutes an area about the size of the United States. It soon became obvious that the spawning grounds of the eel were situated somewhere in this area.

All adult eel die soon after spawning in the depths of the Sargasso Sea. The small eel larvae, which hatch at the great depth of about 1,000 metres, are then carried by the warm Gulf Stream towards the European continent. Their journey lasts the whole of three years. After this the tiny transparent *Leptocephalus* change into the small elvers, which only then become capable of swimming against the sea and river currents.

The male eel continues to live in mixed fresh and sea water in the river estuaries, whilst the females travel inland upstream. This journey is long and tiring because they have to overcome large obstacles and battle against a strong current. Nevertheless they grow faster than the small males. The females stay inland for a number of years. When they stop growing, they return to the sea and rejoin the males in the river estuaries. They then swim back to the Sargasso Sea, where they began their journey so many years before in the form of the small and transparent *Leptocephalus*. This outline description still remains the only certain information of the eel's migratory habits.

American eel, which are born to the west of the European eel, cover a much shorter distance during their journeys in the sea and grow faster than the European eel. They reach the North American sea shore as early as the autumn in their first year of life and the following spring the females migrate upriver. From this point their pattern of life is similar to that of the European eel.

EARLY LIFE OF A FISH

When the fish fry hatches from the egg, it barely resembles the adult fish at all. In its larval stage the freshly hatched fish embryo is usually transparent, a matter of millimetres long, with a large yolk sac on its underside. During the first few days after hatching it lives off this yolk so that it need not look for food. The head of the small fish embryo is usually equipped with a special sticky gland, which enables it to adhere firmly to any adjacent water vegetation, to stones or other objects in the water. At first the small fish usually remains hanging from such plants or rests on the bottom. It only starts to swim about freely and catch food after several days, but occasionally in certain species this can take even longer, until in fact the yolk sac is fully absorbed. At this stage its food consists of the smallest invertebrates which float freely in the water, that is animal plankton. This consists of small water crustaceans, such as the larval stages of daphnia and cyclops, small rotifers and the young larvae of water insects. Only after the yolk sac is completely used up does the fry begin to resemble its parents. The pectoral fins are in fact well developed as soon as it hatches, but the original continuous fin edging only begins to divide into individual single fins later. Its ventral fins also start to grow, its mouth becomes a distinct shape and its body starts growing scales. After this they grow very fast and are sexually mature sometimes as early as the end of their first year of life, though more frequently it is in their second, third or even later years that they begin to breed. It is interesting to note that the males usually mature earlier than the females.

In the early stages of its existence the fish fry has a large number of enemies. It is attacked by the large, carnivorous larvae of water insects, by other water invertebrates and also by many larger fish, often even by its own parents. For example the most dangerous enemies of the small members of the carp family are the young offspring of predatory fish, which have usually hatched several weeks earlier and are thus partly grown before the others spawn.

The survival of some of these tiny fishes during the earliest and the most dangerous days of their life is ensured by their production in large quantities. A single carp female usually has about one million eggs and some fish species produce even more. The most fecund freshwater fish is the large beluga, as one large female of this species can lay as many as five million eggs in a single spawning.

The larval stages of some fish are sometimes so distinctive in shape and so different in form from the adult fish, that they were considered for a long time to be independent species. The history of one such fish, the eel, has already been mentioned and other examples can now be introduced. For example, the larvae of the parasitic lamprey, sometimes called prides, differ considerably from the adult fish, if studied closely. Like the adult fish, they have a snake-like body, but they have no suction disc at the front of their body and are completely blind, whilst their mouth is margined by very fleshy lips. Their way of life also differs significantly; they live in the mud of streams and rivers and feed on organic remnants and diatoms. Even more remarkable is that in some types of lamprey, the larvae are in fact bigger than the adult fish.

Similarly unusual is the development of the European flounder. The newly hatched fry are completely symmetrical and resemble the embryos of other fish. They are deep-bodied, they have a long fin edging, quite a sizeable yolk sac and their eyes, like those of other fish, are located on both sides of their head. They also swim in the water in the same manner as other fry. It is only after several weeks that their way of life and the shape of their body begin to change significantly. Increasingly they incline to one side of their body, so that they reach a stage when they are swimming on one side all the time. During this period of their existence they also leave the top layers of water and move towards the bottom, which becomes their permanent home. This change in their pattern of life brings about a gradual change in the shape of their body. The origi-

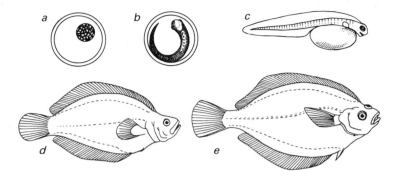

Fig. 6. Development of the European flounder: a) egg, b) spawn with an embryo, c) alevin or larva, d) young fish still at symmetrical stage, e) fish undergoing asymmetrical development.

nally symmetrical bone structure of their head begins to develop asymmetrically, resulting in a gradual movement of one eye to the other side of the head so that eventually both eyes are positioned on that side of the body which is permanently turned away from the river bottom. This side therefore definitely becomes the top side; it turns a darker colour, while the eyeless side remains white.

The characteristic feature of all European flounder and their relatives (such as the sole and the plaice) is their ability to change colour. They can readily and perfectly adapt the colour of the top side of their body to the predominant colour of their environment, so that they blend into it. They can reproduce not only plain shades of grey, black, yellow or brown, but even multi-coloured patterns. A similar ability to change colour, though on a much smaller scale, is also shared by some other central European fish. The most famous 'chameleon' of mountain streams is the trout. When swimming above a yellow, sandy bed, the colour of its back is pale, while above dark-coloured stones at the bottom of pools it turns almost black. During the first days of their life the embryos of the majority of central European fish remain in shallow water close to the banks and especially in water warmed by sunshine and containing a plentiful supply of suitable food. Here they cannot be seriously threatened by larger carnivorous fish. However, the embryos of predatory fish, such as young pike, soon develop cannibalistic traits. A larger specimen of a young pike often eats its smaller brothers and sisters. Sometimes such a young pike under-estimates its prey and attacks a fish which is too big to be swallowed. The normal outcome is that both the hunter and the hunted die. Similar behaviour is characteristic of the young offspring of other predatory fish, such as the trout and the zander.

HOW AND WHAT FISHES EAT

The majority of fish are carnivorous, but this does not mean that all fish prey only on other fish or equally large water vertebrates. The most usual fish food consists of a variety of bottom-living and mid-water organisms, such as insect larvae, molluscs, small planktonic crustaceans, etc. The carp is a typical bottom feeder and they can often be seen in the shallows of ponds or lakes. Every now and then some of them remain motionless in the water, stretching their heads down to examine the bottom. Then the carp opens its fleshy lips and sucks in a volume of water, mud etc. with an often audible sucking noise, which results in the clouding of the nearby area. Then it moves back a little, adopts its usual position, opens its mouth and after a while spits out a cloud of fine mud and crushed vegetation.

When a large shoal of barbel is discovered in a river usually under tree branches or under overhanging banks they can be approached and even tickled on the belly without their apparently being disturbed. Only if a fish is prodded a little harder does it lash out its strong tail, move a little forward and again become motionless facing upstream. It is most interesting to watch barbel when they search for food on the river bed. They can actually move relatively large stones with their fleshy nose and enjoy eating the tiny water animals which hide under them. At the same time they cloud the water with mud, which is then carried away by the current and which attracts other fish species, such as the chub, gudgeon, dace and perch, which in turn also examine its contents.

Many species of freshwater fish live on plankton. Those which live predominantly on plankton, such as the whitefishes, have very dense and long gill filaments; they constitute a very fine sieve which traps even the finest water organisms. Some fish live on insects which fall onto the water surface. This can best be seen by observing trout in mountain streams. During the season when mayflies and caddis flies are swarming, they do not touch any other food. The fish idle in the current close to the water surface and as soon as a fragile insect body touches it, they jump swiftly out of the water with their mouths wide open.

Fish species which catch insects near the water surface include the grayling, the dace, the orfe, the bleak and the asp. Each of these fish has its distinctive method of approaching its prey. The grayling, the dace and the bleak usually pull insects gently below the water surface and then eat them, as opposed to the chub and the orfe, which suck in insects swimming on the surface, whilst the asp and the trout snap at them.

Large predatory fish, such as the pike, which consume large morsels of food, follow a different pattern of hunting. They wait motionless in hideouts under the roots of trees and in the deep shade of a bank or a boat. If a small fish appears, the pike turns slowly after it almost without being noticed. Then comes a sudden movement, and the pike disappears. Later it can be seen again, already with the prey in its mouth. Before the pike catches up with its prey, it opens its mouth wide, so that a stream of water can freely flow through its gills and out. Usually it catches the small fish across its length and only seldom manages to catch it headfirst. After that, it usually remains still for a moment and then starts to squeeze the trapped fish with quick, short movements of its large jaws. Its prey at first squirms and tries to get away, but after a while it becomes motionless. Only at this moment does the pike change its position so as to direct the head of its captive down into its gullet. If the prey is small, it disappears in a moment into the pike's stomach. However, if the pike has attacked a larger fish, it often takes a long time to swallow it.

The pike is a solitary fish and always hunts independently, but other predatory fish are often more sociable creatures. The zander and the perch, particularly when they are young, hunt their prey in shoals. Only large and old fish of these species hunt individually, in the same manner as the pike. Small perch attack roaming fish fry from the water depths in a sort of swarming formation. Sometimes such predatory fish, in the excitement of the chase, find themselves almost on dry land and then a great effort is needed to return to the safety of deep waters. While perch hunt rather close to the water surface, the zander prefer deeper waters, but even here such fish tend to swim in schools.

The diet of large trout also consists of fish and in the same way as other predators they also attack small fish of their own species. However, the favourite food of the trout are the minnow and the bullhead. It is not difficult for the trout to catch a minnow, but the bullhead often proves a more difficult prey. It likes to hide under stones and in very small crevices, where the trout cannot get at it. On the other hand, a trout often patiently waits until the bullhead leaves its safe hideout and then attacks it as soon as it starts to dart over the river bed.

The asp and the chub, which usually hunt just below the surface, are unrestrained hunters of small fish. They usually prey on bleak, roach and rudd and often dart into a shoal of fish, creating a tremendous disturbance in the water. They are voracious and no sooner have they caught a fish, than it disappears down their gullets.

However, the most dedicated hunter is the huchen, the queen of the submountainous reaches of the River Danube and its tributaries. Its favourite food consists of large fish, which it often pursues so wildly that the water in the pool begins to churn, as if subject to a strong storm. It regularly hunts the silvery, shimmering nase. The wels is similarly disturbing on its hunting expeditions; it lives in deep water, where it likes to hide under an uprooted tree, an overhanging rock or in the shadow of a stone, and hunts its prey near the surface at night. The opportunity for the author to watch a hunting wels only occurred once, when the original purpose of the expedition was to photograph roach and bream living in a large overgrown part of the River Danube. During a patient wait on the river bed for the expected arrival of fish, a large wels suddenly appeared from the heart of the plant undergrowth and darted into a shoal of carefree fish. When the wels rolled over near the water surface, and created waves in the water, it was already holding a sizeable bream in its large mouth, which it immediately swallowed. In a flash the large predator had as quickly disappeared into the water depths. This was the only occasion when the writer saw a wels openly hunting during the day.

Some species of freshwater fish, such as the adult rudd, live exclusively on vegetation. The food of very young rudd consists of small animal plankton, but when they are about seven centimetres long, they become vegetarians and live on pondweed, stonewort and other soft aquatic vegetation. Even the carnivorous carp likes to eat water plants, whilst the silvery, shimmering nase in the submountainous tributaries of the Danube can often be seen scraping algae from submerged stones which often contain tiny animals.

Another well-known herbivorous fish, which has been recently imported to central Europe, and for experiment, to the British Isles and parts of the United States, is the grass carp (*Ctenopharyngodon idella*), which is a member of the carp family. Its native land is China and the watershed of the River Amur in the Soviet Union. It has also been reared experimentally in some ponds, where it has been given a supplementary diet of clover, lucerne and other nutritious plants. Sometimes it escapes from these ponds into open waters even though it is a large fish weighing over thirty kilograms.

By way of conclusion, it should be noted that fish form a link in an intricate food system in which man also plays an important part. The problems of fish food and diet are in this way closely connected to the problems of food and nutrition faced by other links in the chain. For man fish is such an important source of protein, vitamins and minerals, that the human diet is difficult to imagine without it.

FISH AND MAN

The nutritional value of freshwater fish for mankind is incomparably smaller than that of sea fish, but by no means negligible. The volume of fish caught every year over the last few decades from seas and oceans has reached roughly forty million tons and only just over a tenth of this is provided by the average world catch of freshwater fish.

Intensive fishing by hooks and nets annually accounts for many fish and because the natural process of reproduction is insufficient, it is necessary to restock with appropriate fish species not only ponds, but also open waters, such as lakes, rivers and reservoirs.

In Europe fish have been reared since the Middle Ages in ponds or artificial reservoirs, which can be periodically emptied and the fish caught. The main species of fish reared in ponds have traditionally been the carp, the zander and the trout, whilst in recent decades even wels and some Asiatic herbivorous fish such as the grass carp have been cultivated.

Pond breeders maintain adequate levels of economically important fish fry in ponds and open waters through artificial and semi-artificial breeding methods. Semi-artificial breeding involves the parent fish being planted in special, small, shallow ponds, which have either densely overgrown or hard, smooth water beds. In the latter case the breeders construct special nests to allow certain fish to spawn. When the fish have spawned onto the plants or into the nests, this is removed and the hatched embryos are gradually transplanted to small, shallow fry ponds, which are rich in nutritional compounds. From here the small fish are often taken as early as the first but sometimes in the second year to larger ponds, rivers, lakes and reservoirs. This method is used in the breeding of the carp, zander and wels. While the carp spawn onto soft, freshly flooded vegetation, the latter two species need nests specially prepared in the

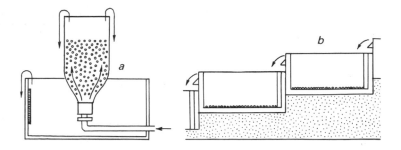

Fig. 7. Fish-hatching equipment: a) Zug bottle for hatching pike, b) Californian apparatus for hatching salmon.

chosen spawning pond. The nests for the zander are usually made of sedge or branches of coniferous trees, whilst the wels favours tree stumps or the tops of dry fruit trees, all of which are interwoven with fine willow roots. This type of substrate is appreciated by such fish and they readily spawn on it.

Other fish, such as the pike, members of the salmon family and whitefishes are bred artificially. Sexually mature specimens are usually removed from open waters or ponds immediately prior to spawning and the spawn and milt are extracted from them by gently pressing the abdominal part of their body. These are then placed in a suitable ratio in special containers where further development takes place under constant supervision and control until finally the tiny fish embryos are hatched. Trout hatcheries are equipped with various types of apparatus for hatching spawn. The two most widespread are those designed to ensure an undercurrent and a constant circulation of water. In the first type a current of water is directed through the bottom of the sieve which contains the spawn and thus the spawn is well rinsed and the hatched embryos are gently lifted up by the water flowing from below and remain undamaged. In the second type of apparatus a permanent circulatory movement of water is provided so that the current flows constantly through the layer of spawn.

The apparatus used for hatching fish belonging to the salmon family is not suitable for hatching pike spawn, because these tend to cluster together and are easily attacked by moulds. Pike, grayling and whitefish are therefore hatched in a container where a constant flow of water from below gently lifts them, disperses them and moves them about all the time. This prevents them from forming clusters and so becoming mouldy and thus dying. The instant disposal of dead mouldy spawn is very easy as they are immediately lighter than healthy spawn, with the result that they are readily washed away by the flow of water. This apparatus used for hatching pike consists of glass containers into which water is introduced from below at a constant pressure, whilst at the top of it the water spills over into an associated container with a fine sieve. This catches not only the dead spawn, but also the hatched embryos. In another similar type of apparatus water is brought to the bottom of a glass container through a tube from above and then flows away through an aperture in the upper part of the apparatus. The pike embryos are carried into this apparatus by the constant undercurrent of water.

Thus by artificial and semi-artificial breeding man assists nature and returns to it what he has taken away. Losses resulting from controlled semi-artificial and artificial spawning are negligible as compared to losses that occur in nature. In open waters any deposited spawn and the tiny fish embryos encounter a great many enemies and their development is dependent on a whole range of factors, such as water temperature, fluctuations in the water level, sudden floods etc. By comparison, the results of semi-artificial and artificial breeding are almost a hundred per cent successful.

Artificially reared fish are transplanted into open waters either in the form of newly hatched embryos or as one- or two-year-old fry. It is obvious that the larger the planted fish is, the higher are its hopes of survival and the avoidance of a number of dangers. With luck the vast majority will grow into a capital catch, which is the wish of every fisherman.

FISH FOOD

1 — small fish inhabiting stagnant waters, 2 — small fish inhabiting mountain streams, 3 — small fish inhabiting lowland rivers, 4 — small fish inhabiting mountain and submountain waters, 5—fish inhabiting top layer of slow-flowing waters, 6 — amphibians, 7 — small mammals, 8 — the young of water birds, 9 — fish spawn, 10 — water snails, 11 — red midge larvae, 12 — mayfly larvae of mountain waters, 13 — adult mayflies of mountain waters, 14 — caddis fly larvae of mountain waters, 15 — stonefly larvae, 16 — adult stonefly, 17 — plankton larvae (*Chaoborus*), 18 — caddis fly larvae of slow-flowing waters, 19 — mayfly larvae of slow-flowing waters, 20, 23 — planktonic crustaceans, 21 — crustaceans of mountain streams (freshwater shrimp), 22 — small planktonic vegetation, 24 — diatoms, 25 — damselfly larvae, 26 — dragonfly larvae, 27-30 — soft, aquatic plant growths.

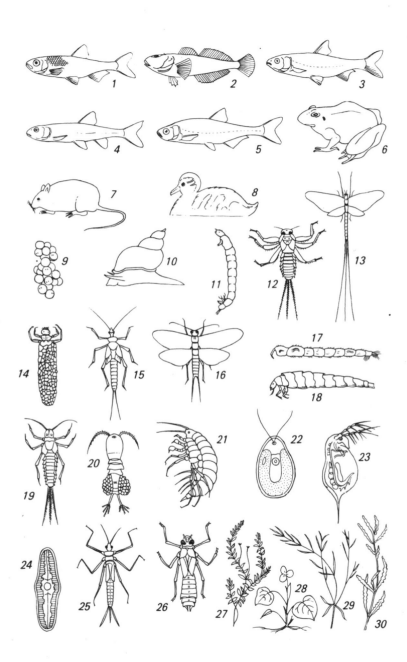

In those cases where the male and female differ in appearance (sexual dimorphism) both are shown, the male being marked with the symbol ♂, the female with the symbol ♀.

The illustrations representing the types of food of the individual species, which are to be found on many plates, are explained on pages 44—45.

Sea Lamprey

Petromyzon marinus

This fish is the largest of the lampreys. Adult specimens, often up to one metre in length, migrate in spring from seas into rivers, where they can be seen from March to June. Between May and July they gather in the shallow parts of the river, where the water current is strong and the bottom covered with stones. With the help of their sucking mouth the females remove stones from the water bed and prepare the spawning ground. The digestive system of adult lampreys degenerates during their journey upriver, so that they cannot eat and die soon after spawning. The lamprey larvae have eyes covered with skin and their mouth is toothless but has distinctive fringed lips. They live in freshwaters in river bottom mud for about four years and then change into adult fish and migrate back to the sea. The mouth of the adult lamprey is funnel-shaped and covered with fine horny teeth; in addition it has a large fleshy tongue, which works in and out like a piston rod. In the sea lamprey live parasitically on various species of fish, sucking their body juices and crushing their muscles, so that they often leave deep circular wounds on the bodies of their prey.

The basic colour of the sea lamprey's body is grey-green with a striking marble-like pattern, whilst the belly is white. It lives close to the European coastline from Scandinavia as far as the eastern shores of Italy. It also inhabits the western Atlantic ranging from Nova Scotia to Florida. It is this lamprey which entered the Great Lakes (through the Welland Canal) and which became a serious pest to the native fishes.

Maximum size and weight: 100 cm, 1 kg. *Identifying characteristics:* Typical teeth coverage of the whole mouth funnel; dorsal fin divided into two parts, the back part of it joined to the caudal fin.

1 – adult fish,
2 – detail of sucker mouth

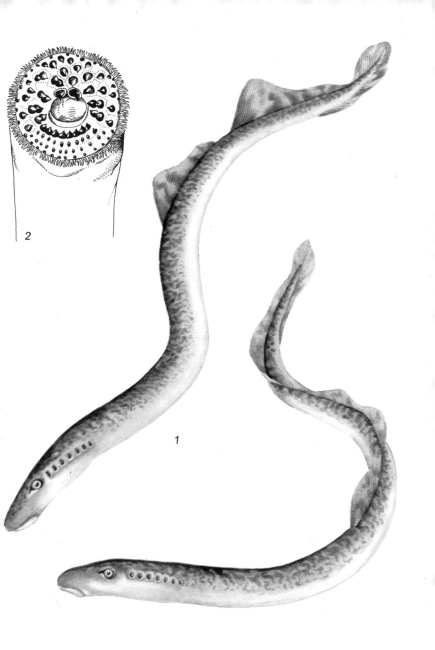

Lampern

Lampetra fluviatilis

Petromyzonidae

The lampern is about 40 cm long, has a dark blue to grey-green back and sides and a silvery white belly. It enters the rivers from the sea between September and November and swims against the current well into the upper reaches of the river. It spawns between February and May. During migration the lampern's body acquires a bronze sheen, it stops eating and dies soon after spawning. The larval stage develops over a period of three to four years; the blind larvae, called prides, lack the suctorial organ and live in the silt deposits on the river bed in quiet backwaters. They feed on any decaying organic matter. When about 15 cm long, they change into typical lampern equipped with eyes and the characteristic funnel-shaped mouth. In March they migrate downstream to the sea and often spawn in the same year that they left freshwaters. They live parasitically on small sea fish.

The lampern is abundant along the European coast from southern Norway to the coasts of Britain and in the Baltic Sea. Its freshwater variety inhabits the Lakes of Ladoga and Onega. In the Mediterranean it lives in the area extending from Spain to Italy. The lampern is economically important in some localities. It is caught during the mass migration period especially in those rivers which flow into the Baltic Sea.

Maximum size and weight: 40 cm, 350 g. *Identifying characteristics:* Funnel-shaped mouth contains characteristic array of large horny teeth. The dorsal fins close together, in the spawning season connected.

1 – adult fish,
2 – ammocoete,
3 – detail of sucker mouth

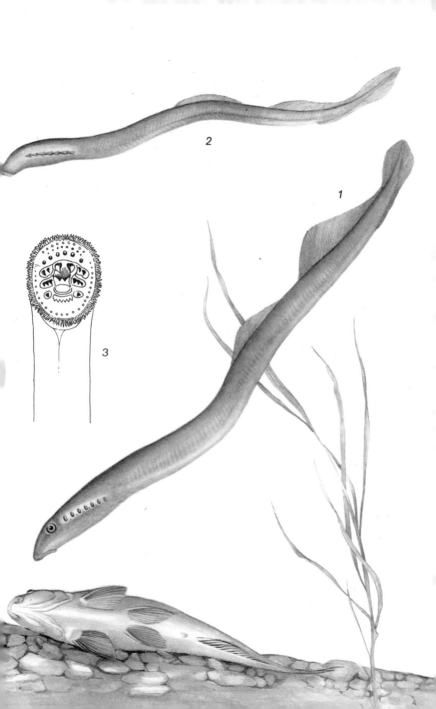

Danube Lamprey

Eudontomyzon danfordi

Brook Lamprey

Lampetra planeri

The Danube lamprey, which is about 20 cm long, inhabits both mountain streams and larger rivers. Prior to spawning both partners dig circular hollows in the sandy bed and into these the female lays her eggs. The male gyrates around her and fertilizes the spawn. The larvae live between four and five years in the sandy, humus deposits and feed on any organic remnants and diatoms. The adult lamprey attacks other fish, at first cutting their skin with its sharp teeth and then feeding on their blood. In contrast to other related species, it usually lives another two to three years after spawning. It lives in the tributaries of the Danube and the rivers flowing into the Black Sea south of the Danube; however, it is not found in the upper reaches of that river.

The small, non-parasitic freshwater brook lamprey is about 15 cm long and spawns from May to June in mountain streams. It can be distinguished from the Danube lamprey by a different teeth arrangement in the funnel-shaped mouth. As in the previous species, the larvae are larger than the adult fish. After reaching adulthood, they develop a sucker disc, their digestive tract is reduced and they mature sexually. Adult brook lampreys die after spawning. The species inhabits the rivers flowing into the North and Baltic Seas and those of north-eastern Italy and Albania.

A similar non-parasitic species, the American brook lamprey *(L. lamothenii)*, lives in the eastern United States.

Eudontomyzon danfordi
Maximum size and weight:
20 cm, 100 g.
Identifying characteristics:
Characteristic arrangement of horny teeth in funnel-shaped mouth. Lives permanently in freshwaters.

Lampetra planeri
Maximum size and weight:
15 cm, 50 g.
Identifying characteristics:
Horny teeth characteristically arranged in the funnel-shaped mouth. Both parts of the dorsal fin connected. Non-migratory.

1 – *Eudontomyzon danfordi*,
1a – detail of mouth funnel,
2 – *Lampetra planeri*,
2a – detail of mouth funnel,
3 – spawning of *L. planeri*

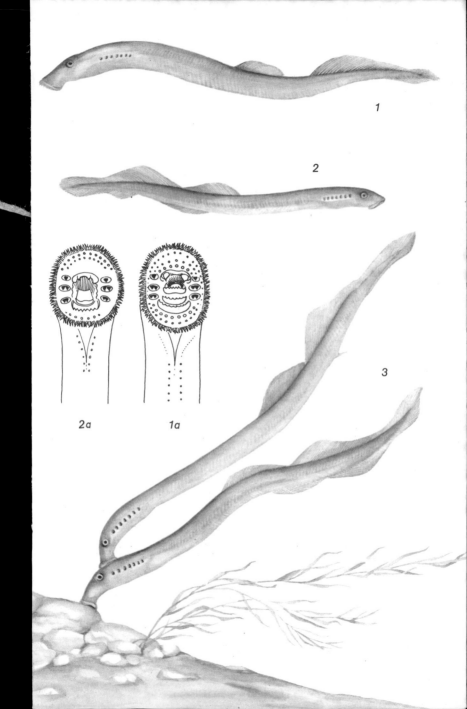

1

2

2a

1a

3

Sturgeon

Acipenser sturio

The sturgeon is a large, migratory fish, weighing sometimes more than three hundred kilograms. It enters the rivers in April and May. Its sides are covered with about 30 plates, the number of the dorsal plates varies from 9 to 13. It spawns between June and July in deep hollows in fast running water. It lays a large number of eggs, which can rise to as much as two and a half million. The adult fish and the embryos stay in freshwater for only a short time. They live on various marine invertebrates, such as crustaceans, worms and molluscs, whilst large sturgeon even hunt fish that live near the sea bed.

It lives along the whole of the European coast from the North Cape as far as the Black Sea. It used to migrate up the Rhine to Basle, up the Elbe and into the Vltava as far as Prague, also up the Oder to Wroclaw and up the Vistula to Cracow. It also lives in the Danube delta but only rarely any higher up that river.

Its economic importance in Europe is negligible, although at the end of the last century it used to be abundant in all large rivers. Its gradual disappearance has been the result of intensive fishing and river pollution, as well as the result of an increasing number of large water constructions, which have made it impossible for the fish to migrate upstream. Its importance at the present time is confined to the area around the Black Sea.

A closely similar species *(A. oxyrinchus)* lives along the American Atlantic coastline from the St. Lawrence to the Gulf of Mexico. It too is now relatively rare.

Maximum size and weight: 300 cm, 300 kg. *Identifying characteristics:* About 30 lateral plates, 9—13 dorsal plates. Barbels not branched, semicircular in cross-section. Snout relatively flat.

1 – adult fish,
2 – larva,
3 – head from side,
4 – head from below

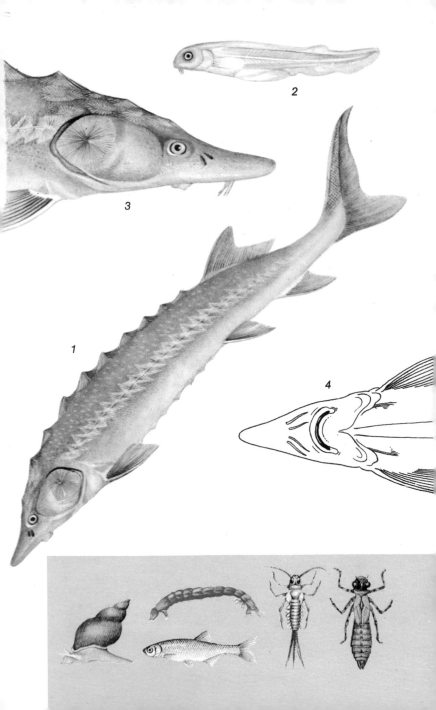

Sterlet

Acipenser ruthenus

This relatively small member of the sturgeon family permanently inhabits freshwaters. It has a long and pointed snout and branched barbels. Like other members of this family, it also lives close to the river bed. It spawns in May in strong currents on a gravelly base, whilst in autumn and spring it congregates in the deep hollows of the river bed. It reaches a length of 125 cm and a weight of 6 to 7 kg. Its diet consists of the larvae of the mayfly, caddis fly and other insects. It has a regional economic importance as it is also reared in carp ponds, where crossbred varieties usually grow faster than the parent species.

It lives in the tributaries of the Black, Azov and Caspian Seas and the Arctic Ocean from the River Ob to the Kolyma. It can also be found in the river estuaries of the Baltic Sea, such as that of the Dvina. In the Danube it reaches as far as the Passau and on rare occasions the rivers Isar and Salzach. Along the coastline and estuaries of the Arctic Ocean it has evolved into an independent species, which differs significantly from the other types of sturgeon found in the river tributaries of the Baltic, Black, Caspian and Azov Seas.

Maximum size and weight: 150 cm, 16 kg. *Identifying characteristics:* Long and pointed snout; long, branched barbels. Back has 11—17 bony plates with long, sharp, hook-like thorns.

1 – adult fish,
2 – larva,
3 – detail of head,
4 – head from below

Allis Shad
Alosa alosa

Twaite Shad
Alosa fallax

The allis shad, belonging to the herring family, has a blue-green back and silvery white sides and belly. The top edge of its gill cover has a black spot, which is usually followed by another one or two less conspicuous spots. It has no lateral line on its sides. In May and June it journeys upriver to spawn, often travelling great distances against the current. Its eggs float above the river bed and the embryos hatch in 3 to 4 days. When the fish is about 8 to 12 cm long, it migrates from the river to the sea. Here it lives several years and feeds on crustaceans. Reaching a length of 30 to 40 cm, it migrates for the first time to spawn in freshwaters. It lives close to the European coasts of the Atlantic Ocean and in the western part of the Mediterranean.

The twaite shad is a migratory herring species, which enters the lower reaches of rivers to spawn in June and July. Its reproductive process and way of life is similar to the former species, although this fish is smaller. It also has a number of black blotches in a line along the sides. During migration it is most numerous in the lower reaches of European rivers. It lives close to the European shoreline in the Mediterranean, in the Atlantic Ocean and in the Baltic Sea as far as the shores of southern Norway, Sweden and Finland. The allis shad and the twaite shad used to be economically important fishes, but today are usually very rare in the majority of European rivers, the allis shad being especially rare.

Similar shads occur on the American Atlantic coast, namely the alewife *(A. pseudoharengus)* and the American shad *(A. sapidissima)* — which has been introduced to the Pacific coast.

Alosa alosa
Maximum size and weight:
70 cm, 2.5 kg.
Identifying characteristics:
A black spot behind the upper edge of the gill cover, sometimes another one or two less conspicuous spots behind.

Alosa fallax
Maximum size and weight:
50 cm, 1 kg.
Identifying characteristics:
A line of black spots behind the head.

1 – *Alosa alosa,*
2 – *Alosa fallax*

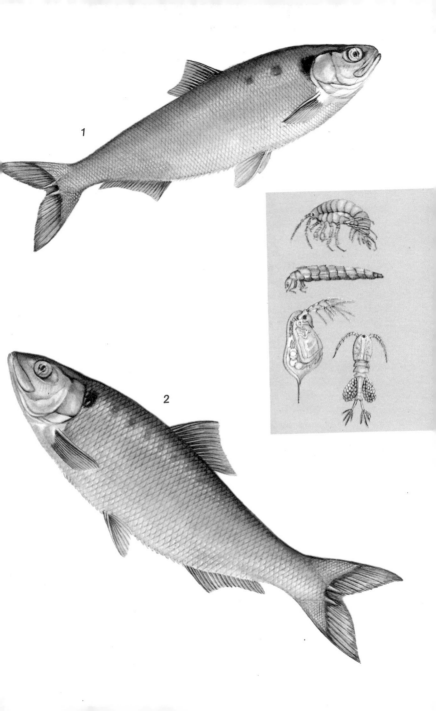

Salmon

Salmo salar

The salmon is a large grey sea fish with black spots shaped like crosses or stars. Its adipose fin is a plain grey. It migrates in the summer and autumn months high upstream against the current to spawn. During migration the males become darker and their sides are decorated with red and orange spots, whilst the belly becomes pink. The females do not change their appearance when they migrate and remain a silvery grey. During their journey they have to overcome strong currents, rapids, weirs and other obstacles as the spawning grounds are located in the upper reaches of rivers in clean and well oxygenated waters. Here the females excavate large hollows (called redds) in which they deposit their eggs which the males fertilize, after which they are covered with gravel. During migration they do not eat and therefore many die after spawning through sheer exhaustion. The young salmon stay in the river for two to three years and only then migrate to sea. They live in the sea one to three years and grow very fast. In freshwaters they feed on small invertebrates, but in the sea solely on fish.

Salmon migrate en masse to spawn in the European rivers extending from the mouth of the Pechora to the rivers of north-western Spain. They are also very numerous in the rivers of Iceland, Greenland and along the Atlantic coast of North America, southwards to the Hudson River. However, during the last century they have become scarcer in a number of European and North American rivers as a result of the construction of irrigation and dam installations and the progressive pollution in the lower rivers and have even disappeared in some.

Maximum size and weight: 150 cm, 50 kg.
Identifying characteristics: Cross- or star-shaped black spots scattered on the sides. Adipose fin plain grey. Upper jaw bone reaches only to the rear of the eye, section of the body in front of tail fin narrow.

1 – adult fish ♂,
2 – detail of head

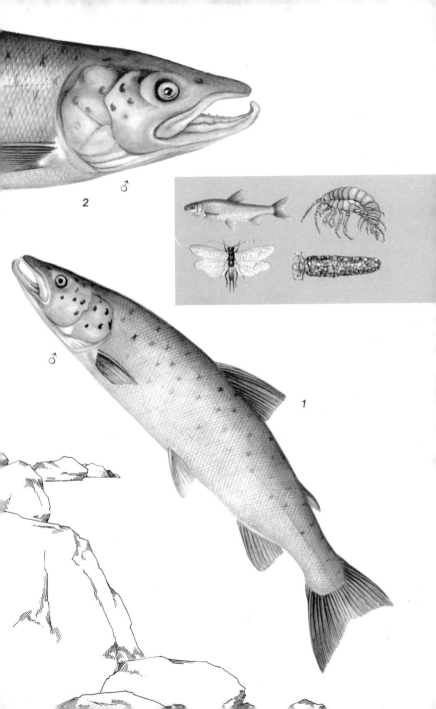

2

1

♂

♂

Salmon

Salmo salar

Salmonidae

The body of the salmon is spindle-shaped, its head is relatively small, its caudal peduncle is quite thin and longer than the anal fin. The caudal fin is slightly curved.

Young salmon, which hatch in spawning grounds in the upper reaches of rivers, usually depart for the sea after two to three years as smolts. Some, however, stay permanently in the river, where they mature sexually, but differ from the sea salmon in their colouring, which resembles that of the trout. They also have 9 to 10 large blue-grey spots on the sides, the parr-marks.

At the final stages of their return journey from the sea to the rivers, salmon are guided by the chemical composition of the water. Every river has for them its individual taste and smell, so that they never make a mistake and always go back to the river where they were born.

In recent years artificial breeding of salmon has been developed in an attempt to counter the losses due to pollution and other factors. Now salmon fertilized eggs and young salmon are put into the rivers in large quantities and so the stock of the salmon is constantly being replaced.

Maximum size and weight: 150 cm, 50 kg.
Identifying characteristics: Cross- or star-shaped black spots scattered on the sides. Adipose fin plain grey.

1 – adult fish ♀,
2 – parr,
3 – parr changing to smolt

1

♀

2

♀

♀

3

Sea Trout

Salmo trutta

The sea trout is one of the large members of the salmon family, which like the salmon migrates upriver to spawn. Its body has a greyish (female) or brownish (male) shade with black or red spots, which often extend along the sides beneath the lateral line. The fish can grow to a length of one metre. Experiments have shown that if sea trout cannot get away from freshwater, they change into brown trout and vice versa, for young brown trout, if put in the sea, will grow into large sea trout, which will then migrate upriver in the spawning period. Because of this the trout is today recognized as a variable species existing in two forms, migratory (the sea trout) and non-migratory (the brown trout), although the distinction is not absolute. The sea trout lives in the same type of waters as the salmon and has a similar economic value, which is realized when they are caught during the migrations upriver.

The sea trout has a bigger head than the salmon, the caudal peduncle is shorter and it is generally high-backed and more robust. Its caudal fin is not curved as in the case of the salmon, but is almost straight. The adult males develop a hook on the lower jaw, just like the salmon.

Maximum size and weight: 130 cm, 40 kg. *Identifying characteristics:* Black and red spots on the sides; upper jaw bone extends beyond the level of the rear of the eye.

1 – adult fish ♀,
2 – adult fish ♂,
3a – shape of operculum of *S. salar*,
3b – shape of operculum of *S. trutta trutta*

1 ♀

♂ 2

3a   3b

Lake Trout

Salmo trutta

The large variety of the trout is especially abundant in mountain lakes and reservoirs. Even today it can be observed that the small brown trout grows into this large lake form when put in such waters. This transformation is accompanied by a change in colouring; this trout acquires a pervasive silvery sheen and has a scattering of black flecks, whilst the red spots, characteristic of the brown trout, disappear. The lake trout grows much faster than the brown trout, it has a high-backed body and is generally more robust. It spawns in the tributaries of lakes and reservoirs together with the brown trout. That part of the trout population which stays in streams, develops into the brown trout, whilst those which move into a lake grow into the larger lake trout. The lake trout usually weighs between 3 and 6 kilograms, but specimens weighing over 30 kg are also known. The young trout live on invertebrates and larger lake trout feed on fish.

The lake trout has a local economic importance in certain areas. It is caught in nets during the migration period and is also valued as an excellent sporting fish by anglers.

Maximum size and weight: 130 cm, 40 kg.
Identifying characteristics: Body coloured a monotonous silver with black spots; red spots lacking.

1 – adult fish ♀,
2 – adult fish ♂

1

♀

2

♂

Brown Trout

Salmo trutta

The brown trout is a typical fish of the salmon family inhabiting mountain streams, rivers and lakes, characterized by its vivid and variable colouring. Immature fish have large, conspicuous grey-blue spots on their sides, while the maturer specimens have small, red flecks, often edged with light shades. The belly is yellow-white to yellow. In autumn and winter it migrates upstream to spawn. The fertilized eggs are deposited by the female into a bowl-shaped depression on the river bed. The size of this trout is closely related to its habitat; in the fast-flowing waters of mountain streams they can reach a length of about 20 cm and weigh about 100 g; however, in lowland rivers rich in food they grow to a length of 60 cm and a weight of about 2 kg. It lives predominantly on water insects and their larvae, as well as other small water animals, whilst the larger specimens often hunt for other fish, including members of their own species.

The brown trout lives in mountain and sub-mountain waters all over Europe, but is differentiated according to the river of its origin. North and Baltic Sea river types are classified as a different subspecies to those originating in the rivers flowing into the Black Sea. However, differences can only be detected after a close anatomical analysis and are not noticeable externally. The brown trout has been introduced to many parts of the world, North America, South America, New Zealand, Australia and elsewhere, on account of its sporting qualities.

Maximum size and weight: 60 cm, 2 kg. *Identifying characteristics:* Back dotted with numerous dark spots; spots on the sides reddish, with lighter edges. Adipose fin light with dark edging and sometimes red at end.

1 – adult fish ♂,
2 – detail of head

1

♂

2

Brown Trout

Salmo trutta

The female of the brown trout has a shorter head than the male and her lower jaw is not curved. During spawning one female is sometimes accompanied by several males. The fertilized eggs are covered with sand and gravel by the female. The trout embryo has a large yolk sac, which is absorbed during the first days of its life. Only then does the fish start to catch its own food, such as insect larvae, young freshwater shrimp, crustaceans, etc.

The economic value of the trout in terms of freshwater fish management is very great indeed. It is one of the most numerous and as such a favourite prey of anglers fishing in mountainous and submountainous waters. In any event, catching brown trout with artificial flies or lures is one of the most exciting experiences for anglers. Experiments in the artificial propagation of the trout have been carried on for centuries. Today many European countries have their own hatcheries, which are the only guarantee that streams will be well stocked with this beautiful fish. The brown trout has also been introduced into cold ponds and even in the warmer waters of open carp ponds, where they grow at a relatively fast rate and are caught in nets.

Maximum size and weight: 60 cm, 2 kg. *Identifying characteristics:* Numerous dark spots on back and sides with additional, light-edged, red flecks on sides. Adipose fin light with dark edging and sometimes red at end.

1 – adult fish ♀,
2 – alevin,
3 – one-year-old fish
4 – two-year-old fish

Rainbow Trout

Salmo gairdneri

Salmonidae

This member of the salmon family comes from the western parts of the USA. It was introduced to Europe in the 1890s and has thrived in some trout waters up to the present day. It is stocked in streams and small rivers, in reservoirs and cold ponds. It spawns mainly in the winter months, but few populations are self-maintaining in Britain. This fish grows very fast where there is plenty of food and sometimes reaches a weight of 1 kg as early as its third year of life. In Europe it can exceed a length of 50 cm and weighs between 4 and 5 kg. It has a bluish or olive-green back and silvery sides with a wide pink or red lateral stripe. The sides, back, dorsal and caudal fins are densely covered with dark spots. Young rainbow trout feed on a range of invertebrates, especially insects both larval and adult, whilst older specimens prey continuously on other fish.

North America as well as Europe is inhabited by non-migratory populations, which live permanently in freshwater. In contrast, other populations of the rainbow trout, called steelheads, have left freshwaters for the sea and only return to the rivers to spawn.

Maximum size and weight: 60 cm, 5 kg. *Identifying characteristics:* Lateral pink or red stripe along silvery sides. Sides, back, dorsal and caudal fins densely covered with dark spots.

1 – adult fish ♀,
2 – adult fish ♂,
3 – young fish

1

♀

3

♂

2

Charr

Salvelinus alpinus

The charr has a blue-green back, grey-blue or greenish sides with small red or orange spots and a glowing red belly. The dorsal and caudal fins are bluish, whilst the others are red. The first rays of the paired fins and the anal fin are white.

This member of the salmon family is of medium size and in the north migrates to spawn in freshwaters. However, many mountain lakes (including some in the British Isles) are inhabited by non-migratory freshwater forms. Breeding takes place either during the late autumn or early spring and the young fish, after hatching, stay in freshwater for three to four years. They migrate to the sea during winter, often swimming under the ice of frozen rivers. Their migration journey can extend into June. During its freshwater existence the charr lives on small fish and insect larvae, but also jumps out of the water to catch flying insects. In the sea it feeds on fish and has a special liking for young herring. It has matured sexually by the time it is six or seven years old.

It inhabits the Arctic seas of Europe, Asia and North America, and the coastal waters of Iceland, Spitsbergen and the northern parts of Norway. However, large numbers of local varieties live in the lakes of England, Ireland and Scotland, in Finnish, Swedish and Norwegian lakes, as well as in the Alps. For example in Lake Constance and other lakes in the Alps a small form with strikingly large eyes can be found in deep waters. The charr is of considerable economic value in the Arctic waters, whilst the lake forms are popular angling fish.

Maximum size and weight: 60 cm, 2.5 kg. *Identifying characteristics:* Blue-green back, grey-blue or greenish sides with small red or orange spots, belly glowing red. First rays of pectoral, pelvic and anal fins white.

1 – adult fish ♂,
2 – adult fish ♀,
3 – deepwater form

Brook Trout

Salvelinus fontinalis

This trout was imported into Europe from North America with other fish species at the end of the last century. In the American populations both permanently freshwater as well as migratory forms are known. The brook trout has an olive back with light marbling pattern and the body covered with red, yellow and blue spots. The fins are pale yellow to reddish, whilst the first rays of its pelvic, pectoral and anal fins are white and black. The biology of the brook trout is similar to that of the brown trout and the charr and thus it can easily be crossbred with them. The hybrids are known as zebra-trout, when crossbred with the trout. It will also hybridize with the Arctic charr. The progeny of both crosses are infertile. It habitually spawns during the winter months when the female excavates a suitable spawning bed. It has a very similar diet to that of the brown trout and the charr.

It has been introduced into some British lakes and in Europe to several Alpine lakes, but has disappeared from many of them. It has only become effectively acclimatized in a few lakes and in some streams high up in the mountains. Generally in Europe it reaches a length of about 50 cm and weighs about 1 kg. However, in North America the brook trout is much larger and heavier and is a popular angling fish.

Maximum size and weight: 65 cm, 3 kg. *Identifying characteristics:* Olive-coloured back with light marbling, red, yellow and blue spots on the sides. Fins pale yellow to reddish; first rays of pectoral, pelvic and anal fins white and black.

1 – adult fish ♂,
2 – starved form from mountain lakes ♂

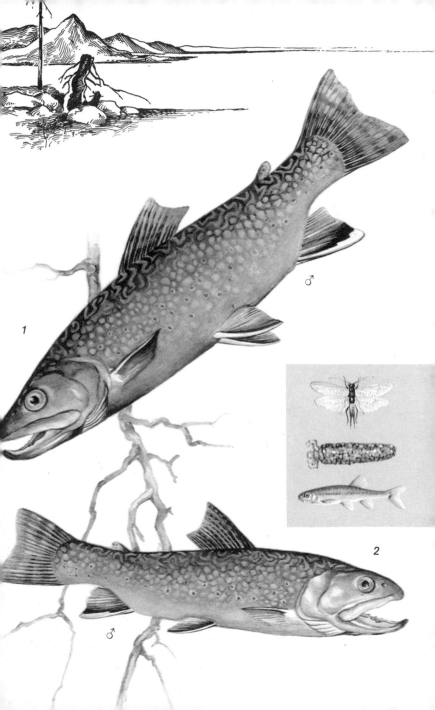

1

♂

2

♂

Huchen

Hucho hucho

The huchen is a large and heavy member of the salmon family, and is a permanent inhabitant of the mountain and submountain reaches of the Danube and its tributaries. It has a long head, slightly flattened on top, and a jaw which extends far behind its eyes. Its back is brownish red or brownish green, often with a purple shade, whilst its sides have a reddish sheen. The belly is white and its sides are dotted with dark spots. Young huchen are silvery in colour and resemble young trout. The huchen spawns in spring at a water temperature of between 6° and 8 °C. Its spawning habits are similar to other members of the salmon family. Young huchen grow very fast; they feed on the larvae of water insects and begin to eat fish already when they are 5 to 6 cm long. In the adult stage huchen catch only fish and other invertebrates. In the River Kama in the European part of the USSR a close relative, the taimen *(Hucho taimen)*, can be found, which achieves an even bigger size.

The huchen is sensitive to water pollution and any oxygen deficiency and therefore in recent years has become extinct in many areas. It is a highly prized angling fish, as specimens weighing up to 10 kg are not exceptional.

Maximum size and weight: 120 cm, 50 kg. *Identifying characteristics:* Long head, slightly flattened from above, jaw reaching behind eyes. Back brownish red or grey-green, sides with reddish sheen and numerous dark spots.

1 — adult fish,
2 — parr stage,
3 — detail of head

Vendace

Coregonus albula

Freshwater Houting

Coregonus lavaretus maraena

The vendace has a relatively short life, usually reaching an age of only five years. It lives in large shoals in lakes and matures sexually in the second or third year of its existence. Its main source of food is plankton. Two subspecies are known, one of which inhabits the watershed of Lake Onega and the other the upper reaches of the Volga. It breeds in November and December and deposits its spawn on the gravelly river bottom at a depth of 2 to 10 metres.

This fish is found in great numbers in the northern lakes around the watershed of the Baltic Sea, whilst in some areas it is also artificially introduced into large reservoirs. It also occurs in a few natural lakes in the Lake District, Scotland and Ireland (where it is known as pollan).

The freshwater houting is a large fish, which in Europe measures up to 130 cm in length and weighs up to 10 kg. It has a dark green back, silvery white sides and belly, and a short snout. It originally came from Lake Madü in Pomerania. As early as 1882 it was introduced into some ponds and since then, it has become an important breeding fish in some areas. It is a deep-water species, which only swims to shallow waters in November, which is its spawning time. It generally lives on plankton but large specimens also catch insects and small fish. A form of *C. lavaretus* occurs in the English Lake District (where it is known as the skelly or schelly), others such as the gwyniad and powan occur in North Wales and south-west Scotland. These fishes never grow to a great size.

Similar whitefishes, also known as ciscoes, are found in North American high altitude lakes.

Coregonus albula
Maximum size and weight:
30 cm, 300 g.
Identifying characteristics:
Relatively slender body, lower jaw longer than upper jaw, mouth in superior position. Caudal fin deeply curved.

Coregonus lavaretus maraena
Maximum size and weight:
130 cm, 10 kg.
Identifying characteristics:
Back dark green, sides and belly silvery white. Snout short and rounded, mouth in inferior position.

1 – *Coregonus albula*,
2 – *Coregonus lavaretus maraena*

Houting

Coregonidae

Coregonus oxyrinchus

Smelt

Osmeridae

Osmerus eperlanus

The houting is a sea fish which lives close to the shores of the eastern North Sea and in the south Baltic. Its body is up to 50 cm long, the snout is pointed and long and the mouth is in the inferior position. The back is blue-green or grey-blue, whilst the sides and the belly are white and the fins a light grey. When about to spawn it migrates into freshwater, where it breeds in November and December on the sandy and gravelly beds of shallow waters. It feeds mainly on plankton and small animals on the river bed. In the southern North Sea the houting is on the verge of extinction. Rivers such as the Rhine, in which it formerly bred, have become so polluted that no fish can survive.

In contrast, the smelt migrates to the upper reaches of rivers to spawn, although it lives generally close to the European coastline from Scandinavia to the English Channel. It is slender with a transparent body, large eyes and a mouth with large teeth. It grows to a maximum length of 30 cm. Its lateral line terminates behind the pectoral fins. The back is green-grey, the sides are a silvery colour and the belly is white. It spawns in March and April in the river. The eggs at first rest on the gravel, but later the outer membrane bursts and the eggs float freely in the river. The larval stage of the smelt is fairly long; only after it has reached a length of 4 to 5 cm, does it develop scales and swim into the sea. Here it lives on plankton, crustaceans and small fish. In certain areas of its habitat it is fished for commercially; its flesh smells of cucumbers.

Coregonus oxyrinchus
Maximum size and weight:
50 cm, 1.5 kg.
Identifying characteristics:
Snout long and pointed, mouth in inferior position. Back blue-green or grey-blue, belly and sides white, fins greyish.

Osmerus eperlanus
Maximum size and weight:
30 cm, 0.5 kg.
Identifying characteristics:
Transparent body, large toothed mouth and large eyes. Lateral line terminates behind pectoral fins. Back green-grey, sides and belly silvery white.

1 – *Coregonus oxyrinchus*,
2 – detail of head,
3 – *Osmerus eperlanus*

1

2

3

Grayling

Thymallus thymallus

The grayling is a schooling fish which inhabits the submountain regions of rivers with sandy or stony beds. It spawns in spring, when it leaves its home territory and migrates upstream to the areas with a more gravelly river bed. The spawning grounds are prepared by the males, which often chase and attract several females onto them. By comparison with members of the salmon family, the grayling has a relatively small head, which has a small mouth with a fleshy, overhanging snout. It has impressively large scales and a high, long and vivid dorsal fin. It measures up to 50 cm and can weigh 1 kg or sometimes even more. The young fish are a light silvery green and often have bluish spots on the sides.

The grayling inhabits the submountain rivers of Europe from Wales and France, across Europe southwards to northern Italy and the watershed of the River Po. However, it is not normally found in southern Europe or the northern parts of Scandinavia and Ireland. In the Alps it swims upriver to a height of 1,500 metres above sea level and in the Carpathians up to about 1,000 metres.

The grayling subspecies *Thymallus arcticus baicalensis*, which is a native of Lake Baikal and its tributaries, has been introduced relatively successfully in some European valley reservoirs. It is distinguished by an overall darker colouring and a larger mouth. Another subspecies is found in North America.

Maximum size and weight: 60 cm, 1.5 kg. *Identifying characteristics:* Fish with large scales, small mouth and adipose fin; dorsal fin strikingly high and brightly coloured.

1 — adult fish ♀,
2 — adult fish ♂

1

♀

♂

2

Pike

Esox lucius

The pike is the only representative of its family to be found in European waters. It has a characteristically depressed head and jaws with large teeth, the dorsal and anal fins are close to the tail fin. The pike has a grey-green or brownish back, greenish sides with yellow spots or stripes and a white belly with light grey spots. Exceptional specimens can reach a length of 150 cm and weigh up to 35 kg. However, pike longer than 1 metre and heavier than 10 kg are quite rare.

It is a predatory fish, which from an early age lives on the fry of other fish and later on adult fish and other aquatic vertebrates. It lives mainly in the lower reaches of rivers, in overgrown river backwaters and pools, but also penetrates high upriver against the current. In waters with a plentiful supply of relatively small fish it grows quite quickly. Its economic value for breeding in ponds as well as in open waters has increased considerably. It is often introduced into carp ponds, where it reduces the supply of small, unwanted fish. In many countries in Europe it is artificially reared and the fry are then relocated in ponds, rivers, dams and lakes. It usually spawns in early spring on the flooded vegetation of river meadows.

It can be found throughout Europe with the exception of the Iberian peninsula, the southern Balkans and southern Italy. Similarly it cannot be traced along the western shores of Norway. It is a species which is indigenous to the temperate and northern zones of the whole northern hemisphere. It is also found in Asia and North America (where it is known as the northern pike).

Maximum size and weight: 150 cm, 35 kg. *Identifying characteristics:* Body long and cylindrical; rearwards placed dorsal fin; large mouth with numerous backward inclined teeth.

1 – adult fish,
2 – alevins,
3 – young fish

1

2

3

Mud-minnow

Umbridae

Umbra krameri

Mottled Black Sea Goby

Gobiidae

Proterorhinus marmoratus

The mud-minnow is a small, reddish-brown, ir-regularly flecked fish with a rounded caudal fin and a lateral line which takes the form of a light stripe along the sides. The head is covered with scales both on the top and sides. It reaches a length of 13 cm at the most and inhabits the basin of the Danube between Vienna and the river's estuary, the lower reaches of the Dniester and Prut, and the lakes Blatenske and Neziderske. It prefers waters overgrown with vegetation and therefore especially frequents irrigation canals, pools, and old river courses. It usually lives for only two years or so, during which time it feeds on small planktonic crustaceans and benthic organisms. Similar mud-minnows are found in silt-bottomed lakes, pools, and even swamps, in North America.

The mottled Black Sea goby is a similarly small, yellow-grey or grey-brown fish, which has several crosswise blotches on its sides and which grows to a length of between 7 and 11 cm. Its pelvic fins are joined together to form a sucker disc, whilst its first dorsal fin has soft spines. Its head is flattened on the top and its front nostrils are prolonged to form tubes, which overhang the upper lip. The lateral line is not developed. The mottled Black Sea goby stays close to the river bed, where it hides amongst the vegetation and lives on small insect larvae and other small invertebrates.

It lives in the brackish waters of rivers opening into the Black Sea, although it can be found in the Danube as far up as the mouth of the River Morava.

Umbra krameri
Maximum size and weight:
13 cm, 30 g.
Identifying characteristics:
Dorsal fin placed well down the back; lateral line forms light stripe on sides. Caudal fin rounded. Head covered with scales on top and at sides.

Proterorhinus marmoratus
Maximum size and weight:
11 cm, 15 g.
Identifying characteristics:
Front nostrils prolonged into tubes overhanging upper lip. Lateral line not developed.

1 – *Umbra krameri,*
2 – *Proterorhinus marmoratus,*
2a – pelvic fins fused into sucking disc in *P. marmoratus*

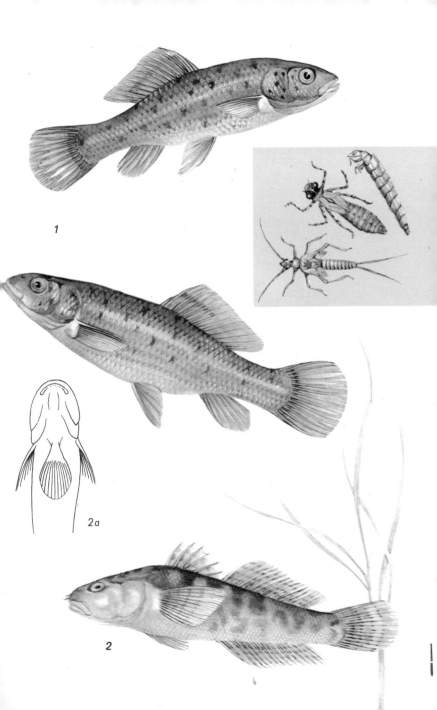

1

2a

2

Roach

Rutilus rutilus

Cyprinidae

The roach, a member of the carp family, is distinguished by its relatively large scales, by the position of the dorsal and pelvic fins, and the angle of its mouth. It has a dark back with a bluish or greenish sheen, the sides are silvery white, the dorsal and caudal fins are grey, other fins reddish in colour. Its dorsal fin is positioned above the base of the pelvic fins. It is a schooling fish and is one of the most prolific species in all types of waters with the exception of the trout zone. It also lives in brackish waters and in the Baltic Sea. The saltwater forms migrate upriver during the breeding season. It usually spawns in April and May in shallow waters on aquatic vegetation. The males have conspicuous hard white pimples on the head and body at this time of the year. In Europe it is locally commercially valuable and is often caught in all types of nets in large reservoirs, ponds, lakes and rivers. In addition, it is a popular angling fish and is used as bait on hooks for catching larger predatory fish. It reaches a length of about 40 cm and may weigh up to 1 kg. In its natural habitat it often interbreeds with other carp species, such as rudd and bream. It feeds on aquatic invertebrates and larger specimens also live on aquatic vegetation.

It can be found all over Europe with the exception of the Iberian and Italian peninsulas, Greece, northern Scotland, much of Ireland and Wales, and northern Norway. Because of its popularity with anglers it is often introduced to new areas.

Maximum size and weight: 40 cm, 1 kg. *Identifying characteristics:* Dorsal fin positioned above the pelvic fin base; body behind the pelvic fins rounded and covered with scales.

1 – adult fish,
2 – alevin,
3 – spawn

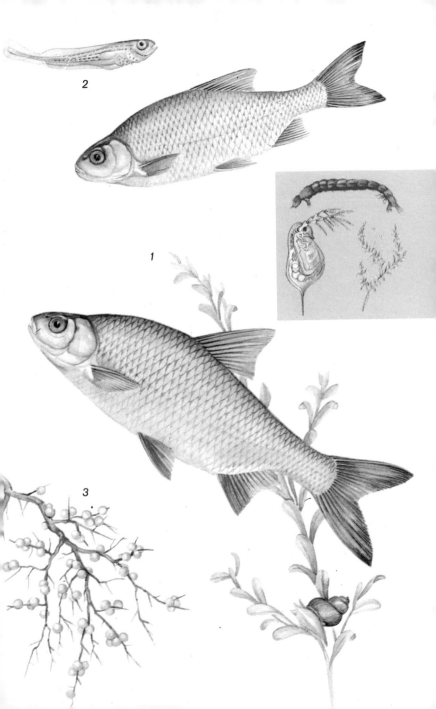

Black Sea Roach

Rutilus frisii meidingeri

Danube Roach

Rutilus pigus

The Black Sea roach has a long cylindrical body, a small mouth and a round protruding snout. Its back is dark brown with a green sheen, its sides are a lighter colour turning to white on the belly. The fins are greyish and transparent. It is a migratory fish, which lives in schools in some German and Austrian lakes within the system of the upper Danube in the Chiemsee, Traunsee, Attersee and Mondsee and their tributaries. It spawns in April and May in the lake tributaries where it feeds on molluscs, worms, insect larvae, plants and small fish. It is often netted during such migrations and is also a popular angling fish. A similar roach *(Rutilus frisii frisii)* is quite plentiful in the north-western river tributaries of the Black Sea.

The Danube roach is a deep-water fish, which can be distinguished from the roach by the higher number of scales in its lateral line and the dark-coloured body tissue in the abdominal cavity. Its scales are relatively large, its mouth occupies a low position on the underside of the head. The dorsal fin is reddish and the caudal fin is a yellow-red. It grows to a larger size than the roach, up to 50 cm in length and about 2 kg in weight. It lives in large north Italian lakes, for example Lakes Maggiore, Lugano, Como and Garda, and is also found in the watershed of the River Po. In the upper and middle reaches of the Danube and its tributaries a subspecies is found, named *Rutilus pigus virgo*.

Rutilus frisii meidingeri
Maximum size and weight:
40 cm, 1.5 kg.
Identifying characteristics:
Body slender and cylindrical; mouth small. Fins greyish and transparent.

Rutilus pigus
Maximum size and weight:
50 cm, 2 kg.
Identifying characteristics:
An opalescent sheen on the sides, dorsal fin reddish, caudal fin red. The body tissue in the abdominal cavity dark.

1 – *Rutilus frisii meidingeri,*
2 – *Rutilus pigus virgo*

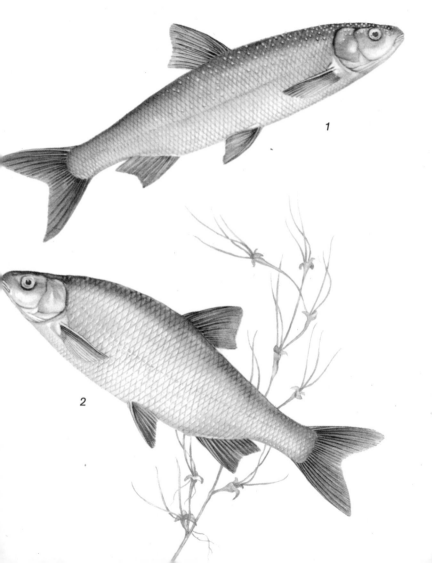

1

2

Moderlieschen

Leucaspius delineatus

Bitterling

Rhodeus sericeus amarus

Moderlieschen has a slender body, flattened at the sides and with easily detached scales. The lateral line is visible only on the first scales towards the front of the body. Its back is greenish, the belly and sides are silvery. It may reach a length of between 7 and 9 cm, although it is usually much shorter. It lives in large schools in stagnant or slow-flowing waters which have become overgrown with vegetation. It spawns in April and May, when the female lays her eggs in strips around the stems of water plants and the male fertilizes and subsequently guards them. Its main diet consists of plankton.

Moderlieschen is indigenous to the whole of central and eastern Europe, from the Rhine as far as the watershed of the Volga; it can be found as far north as the rivers of southern Sweden.

The bitterling is a small fish with a high-backed body. On its sides it has a blue-green stripe, which widens out towards the tail. It is quite abundant in the stagnant waters of the lower reaches of rivers, in shallow creeks, in old river backwaters and pools. However, it lives only in waters inhabited by the freshwater mussel, into which the bitterling lays its eggs between April and June. During this period the male becomes reddish-purple at the sides and the female develops a pink ovipositor by means of which she places the eggs within the mantle cavity of the mussel.

It is found all over Europe from north-eastern France as far as the Caspian Sea, but is not present in Denmark, Scandinavia, or the Mediterranean countries. It has been introduced into a number of waters in north-west England. It lives on planktonic crustaceans, insect larvae and worms.

Leucaspius delineatus
Maximum size and weight:
9 cm, 10 g.
Identifying characteristics:
Mouth slants upwards, scales large and easily shed. Lateral line developed only on the first 7—13 scales.

Rhodeus sericeus amarus
Maximum size and weight:
8 cm, 15 g.
Identifying characteristics:
A blue-green stripe on the sides, widening towards the back. During mating female with long ovipositor, male reddish-purple on sides. Mouth in semi-inferior position; lateral line extends to only 5—6 scales.

1 – *Leucaspius delineatus*,
2 – *Rhodeus sericeus amarus* ♂,
3 – *R. sericeus amarus* ♀

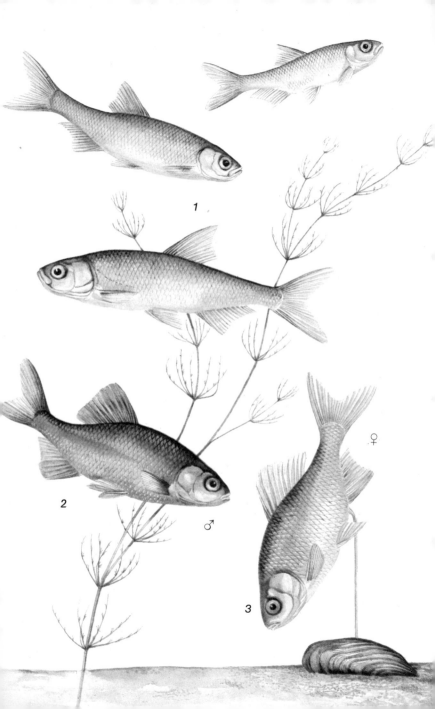

1

2

3

♂

♀

Souffie

Leuciscus souffia

Dace

Leuciscus leuciscus

The souffie is a small fish with a long cylindrical body and an inferior-positioned mouth. A dark wide stripe extends along the whole length of its sides from the mouth to the caudal peduncle, the scales of its lateral line are orange. It is a schooling fish in rivers of the grayling zone and some lakes. It spawns in places with a stony bed and a fresh current of water. During the spawning season both sexes develop white tubercles on head and body. It feeds on small water invertebrates and insects which have fallen into the water. It lives in the watershed of the rivers Rhône and Po *(Leuciscus souffia souffia)*, whilst a subspecies, *Leuciscus souffia agassizi*, inhabits the tributaries of the upper Rhine and the Danube and rivers associated with the watershed of the Tisza.

The dace is a small yet slender member of the carp family, whose body is almost circular in cross-section. It has a dark back with a blue sheen and silvery sides. It can be distinguished from the very similar chub by its small mouth and concave edge to the anal fin. It lives in clear waters of submountainous and lowland rivers and streams and feeds on insects and their larvae, which it collects from the river bed as well as from the surface. From March to May it spawns on aquatic vegetation. It is found in the whole of Europe with the exception of all three south European peninsulas (i. e. Spain, Italy and Greece), Scotland and the northern parts of Scandinavia.

Leuciscus souffia
Maximum size and weight:
20 cm, 100 g.
Identifying characteristics:
Wide dark stripe along the sides from mouth to caudal peduncle. Lateral line scales orange. Mouth in inferior position.

Leuciscus leuciscus
Maximum size and weight:
35 cm, 250 g.
Identifying characteristics:
Mouth small, anal fin edge concave. Lower part of body, behind ventral fins, rounded and covered with scales.

1 – *Leuciscus souffia agassizi*,
2 – *Leuciscus leuciscus*

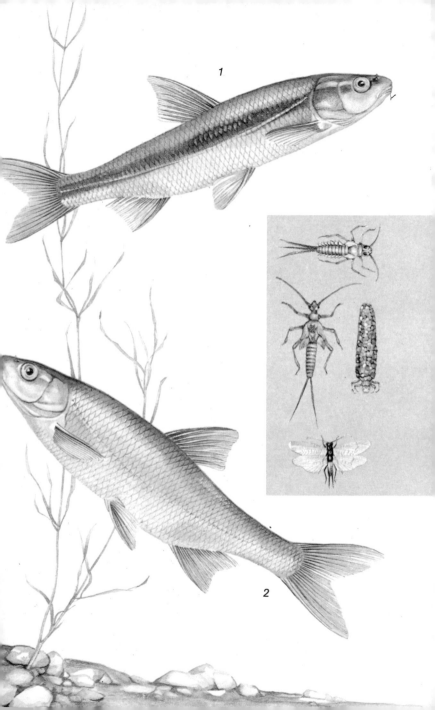

Chub

Cyprinidae

Leuciscus cephalus

The chub is a large fish, often reaching 80 cm in length and over 3 kg in weight. It has a large, wide mouth and a long, cylindrical body with large scales, which are edged in grey or black. The dorsal and caudal fins are greyish-green, whilst the rounded anal fin and the pelvic fins are orange red. It lives in all types of running water from the lower reaches of the trout zone to the lowlands. It usually seeks out shallow waters with a hard bed but can also be found in stagnant waters. It feeds on small invertebrates, insects, small fish, frogs and crayfish, but also eats small fruit which has fallen into the water, and which is occasionally used as bait by anglers. It spawns from April to June on aquatic vegetation and stones. Young chub are gregarious creatures as opposed to older specimens, which are often loners.

This fish can be found in an area stretching from southern Scotland, eastern Wales, and England to the Urals. However, it does not occur in Ireland, Denmark, northern Scandinavia and the Mediterranean islands. It has several sub-species in Europe and its local commercial value is quite substantial as it is caught in all types of nets. Anglers catch it by using plugs, small fish, worms, bread and fruit.

Maximum size and weight: 80 cm, 4 kg. *Identifying characteristics:* Mouth large and wide, anal fin edge rounded, scales with dark edging, forming web-like pattern on the body.

1 – adult fish,
2 – detail of head

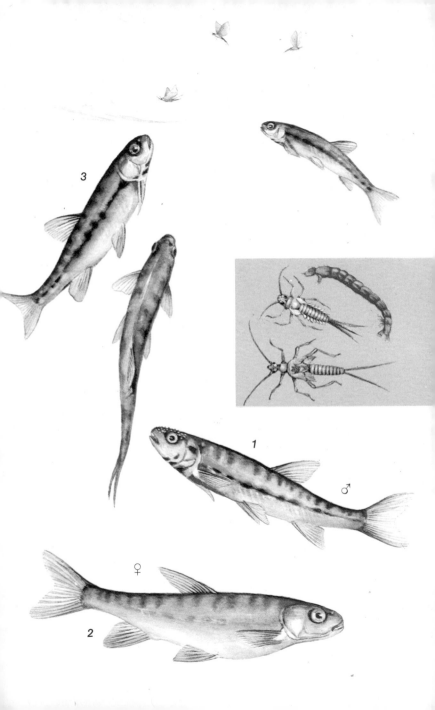

Rudd

Scardinius erythrophthalmus

The characteristic feature of this fish is its scale-covered, sharp keel on the belly, behind the pelvic fins. In some respects it resembles the roach, but is distinguished by the position of its dorsal fin, the origin of which is behind the pelvic fin base. The body is flattened at the sides and its small mouth is oblique. The back is blue-green and the belly a silvery white. Apart from the reddish-grey dorsal and pectoral fins, all other fins are a deep red, whilst the eyes are yellow to yellowish-red. It lives in backwaters in the lower river reaches and in enclosed pools, often those which are profusely overgrown with aquatic vegetation, where it swims about in small shoals. It spawns in May and June on submerged water vegetation. The young rudd, up to 7 cm long, feed on plankton, whereas the larger fish feed mainly on aquatic vegetation, insects and aquatic vertebrates.

With the exception of the Iberian peninsula, Scotland, western Norway, northern and central Sweden and the Crimea, this fish lives all over Europe. A subspecies, *S. erythrophthalmus scardafa*, can also be found in central and southern Italy and Dalmatia. However, its value as a food fish is relatively insignificant although it is popular with anglers.

Maximum size and weight: 30 cm, 1 kg.
Identifying characteristics: A sharp, scale-covered keel behind pelvic fins. Mouth moderate and strongly oblique (tilted upwards). Dorsal fin starts behind imaginary vertical line projected upwards from pelvic fins.

1 – adult fish,
2 – young fish

1

2

Asp

Aspius aspius

The asp has a long body and a wide mouth, which extends behind its eyes. Its upper jaw has a small depression into which the protruding lower jaw fits. It has a grey-blue back and silvery sides. Its dorsal fin is placed behind the imaginary vertical line projected from the base of the pelvic fins. Behind its pelvic fins it has a scale-covered keel.

The asp is a predatory fish, which inhabits the lower reaches of large rivers and sometimes also lives in oxbow lakes. It prefers upper water layers, where it feeds on small fish, which it often attacks noisily, sometimes even jumping out of the water. It also catches insects fallen onto the water surface. It spawns between April and June on the stony bed against the current. The fry at first eat plankton, small insect larvae, the fry of other fish, and later progress to a diet of small fish.

In Europe it inhabits rivers to the east of the Elbe and those opening into the Baltic, Black and Caspian Seas. It is not found in France, Britain, Denmark, Switzerland, the Iberian peninsula or in the southern part of the Balkan peninsula. Its economic value grows proportionately as one moves eastwards through Europe, where it is also a favourite prey of anglers.

Maximum size and weight: 1.2 m, 14 kg. *Identifying characteristics:* Upper jaw has depression into which slots protruding lower jaw. Large mouth reaches behind eyes. Scale-cevered keel behind pelvic fins.

1 – adult fish,
2 – detail of head

1

2

Tench

Tinca tinca

The tench, a sturdy fish, is distinguished by its scales, which are very firmly rooted in the skin. At each corner of its mouth there is a small barbel. The tench's eyes are unusually small. The back is brown-green, the sides have a golden sheen and the belly is creamy-yellow. It is one of the few European fishes whose sex can be recognized at first sight, for the males have longer and stronger pelvic fins than the females. The tench lives in slow flowing rivers, in old river backwaters and oxbow lakes, where the water is often overgrown with vegetation. However, it is also artificially reared in carp ponds. It generally stays close to the bottom, where it feeds on small vertebrates. It spawns prolifically at the end of May and in June on water plants. In cold or very warm seasons it stops eating and buries itself in the mud; so it can tolerate very low oxygen levels in the water. In northern Germany, France and some other countries the tench is a favourite delicacy and is economically very important. It is dispersed all over Europe with the exception of the northern parts of Scandinavia and the USSR, Scotland, Dalmatia and the Crimea. However, it can also be found in the eastern part of the Baltic Sea.

Maximum size and weight: 60 cm, 6 kg. *Identifying characteristics:* Scales small and firmly rooted in skin. Fins rounded, eyes small; two small barbels at the corners of mouth.

1 – adult fish,
2 – ♂ from below,
3 – ♀ from below

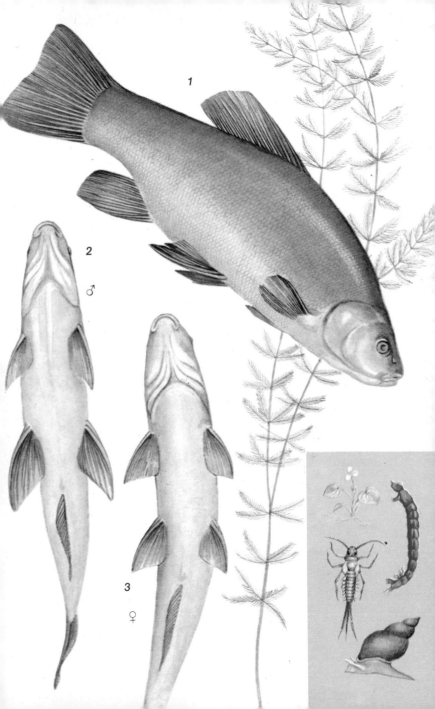

1

2

♂

3

♀

Nase

Cyprinidae

Chondrostoma nasus

The nase is a medium-sized fish with a large body, which is slightly flattened at the sides, and a typical inferior-positioned mouth. Its lips are covered with a horny skin and therefore its mouth has sharp edges. The nase has a grey-blue to grey-green back, silvery sides and belly. All fins except the dorsal fin are red. It usually reaches a length of 40 cm and a weight of 1 kg. It lives gregariously in the middle reaches of rivers and lakes and from these it migrates in shoals upriver to the upper reaches. The nase feeds on algal growths, scraped from stones with their horny lips, leaving characteristic scratch marks on the surface of such submerged stones.

The nase inhabits those rivers which from mainland Europe open into the North and Baltic Seas, and from the north and west into the Black Sea. It can also be found in tributaries of the Caspian Sea. Besides *Chondrostoma nasus*, there are in Europe another seven species of the nase. In northern Italy it is *C. soetta*, in the Iberian peninsula *C. polylepsis*, in northern and central Italy *C. genei* and in the watershed of the river Rhône, Loire and rivers of northern Spain *C. toxostoma*.

Maximum size and weight: 50 cm, 2.5 kg. *Identifying characteristics:* Typical inferior-positioned mouth with sharp edges. Body slightly flattened at sides; sides silvery.

1 – adult fish,
2 – detail of head,
3 – head from below,
4 – young fish

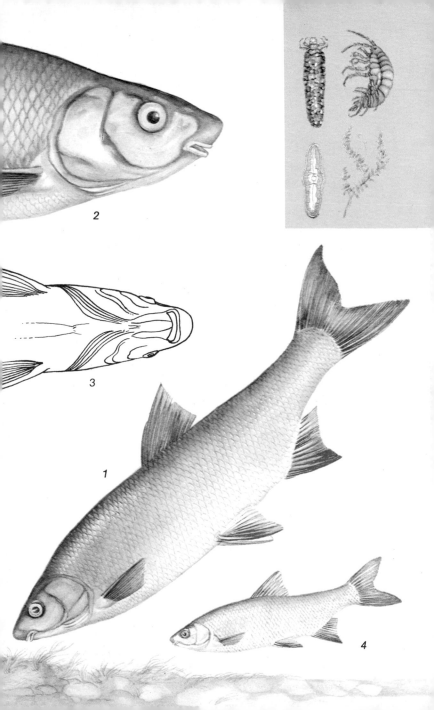

2

3

1

4

Danube Gudgeon

Cyprinidae

Gobio uranoscopus

Gudgeon

Gobio gobio

The Danube gudgeon is a small fish with an elongated, spindle-shaped body, which is covered by quite large scales. It has short dorsal and anal fins and a brownish back with dark spots which become purple or blue at the sides. The mouth is ventral or back behind the head and two long barbels at the sides extend far behind its eyes. The nape is covered with scales. It swims against strong currents and generally lives close to the river bed. It can be encountered in the trout zone and is native to the upper and central parts of the Danube and its tributaries, such as the Isar, and also in rivers of the Carpathian Ukraine and Rumania.

The gudgeon resembles very much the Danube gudgeon, but the two barbels at the corners of its mouth are much shorter and do not reach as far as the eyes. Also the nape in this species is smooth and scaleless. It lives close to the bottom of all types of water. It breeds in May and June spawning in shallow waters on stones and plants. The young fry keep together in schools. It is indigenous to the whole of Europe with the exception of the Iberian peninsula, the southern parts of Italy (although it frequents the watershed of the Po), Greece, Norway, northern Sweden, Finland and Scotland. It is a favourite bait used by anglers for catching predatory fish.

Gobio uranoscopus
Maximum size and weight:
12 cm, 50 g.
Identifying characteristics:
Long barbels touch rear gill-cover bones. Nape covered with scales. Purple to blue spots on sides.

Gobio gobio
Maximum size and weight:
20 cm, 100 g.
Identifying characteristics:
Barbels relatively short, nape scaleless.

1 – *Gobio uranoscopus*,
2 – *Gobio gobio*

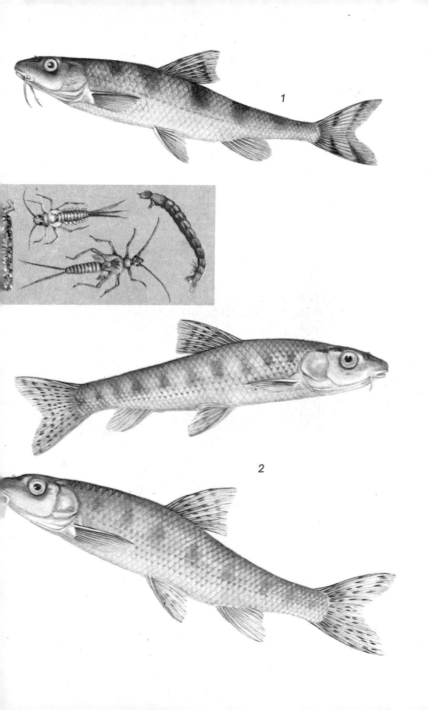

1

2

Barbel

Cyprinidae

Barbus barbus

Southern Barbel

Barbus meridionalis

The barbel grows up to 1 m in length and is a sturdy fish. It lives close to the river bed in strong currents and has a long, spindle-shaped body and a characteristically inferior-positioned mouth with four barbels. The long spine in the dorsal fin has a saw-like edge. The long rayed anal fin nearly reaches the tail fin. It spawns in May and June and migrates upstream to areas with a sandy or stony water bed. It is a schooling fish and feeds on the animals and plants of the water bed.

It inhabits western and central Europe, but is not found in Ireland, Denmark, Scandinavia and Italy. In the peripheral areas of its habitat it has produced numerous subspecies, for example in Spain, Dalmatia, eastern Bulgaria and the watersheds of the rivers Dniester, Dnieper and Bug.

The southern barbel is a smaller fish, which grows to a length of about 30 cm. This also lives close to the river bed amongst strong, clean currents. The large spine in the dorsal fin is smooth-edged, the anal-fin is high and when depressed it touches the tail-fin base.

It is confined to certain areas in the northern part of the Iberian peninsula (which is also inhabited by its subspecies *B. meridionalis graellsi*), southern France, northern Italy, Albania and Greece. Another subspecies *B. meridionalis petenyi* lives in the rivers Oder, Vistula, Danube, Dniester, Vardar, Strymon and Maritsa.

Barbus barbus
Maximum size and weight:
1 m, 15 kg.
Identifying characteristics:
Long spine of dorsal fin has serrated edge. Anal fin does not reach caudal fin. Mouth ventral, with four fleshy barbels.

Barbus meridionalis
Maximum size and weight:
30 cm, 500 g.
Identifying characteristics:
Long spine in dorsal fin smooth. High anal fin reaches tail fin when depressed.

1 – *Barbus barbus*,
2 – detail of head,
3 – *Barbus meridionalis petenyi*

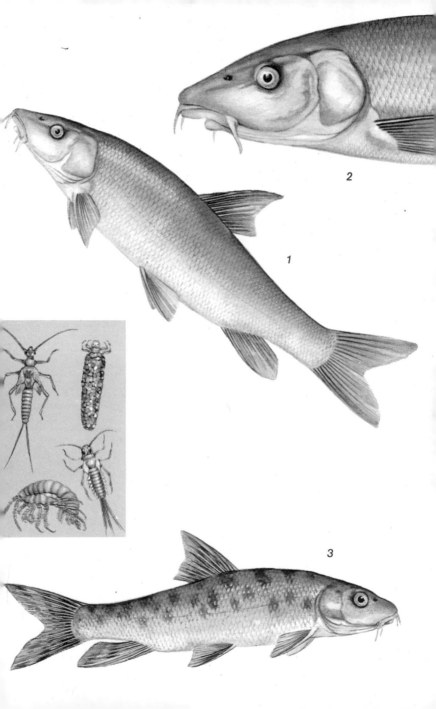

Bleak

Alburnus alburnus

Schneider

Alburnoides bipunctatus

The bleak is a small fish which averages a length of about 15 cm. It has a steeply angled mouth and easily dislodged scales. Its back is green-grey or green-blue, the belly and sides are silvery, whilst the fin bases are yellowish. Its belly behind the pelvic fins forms a keel, which is smooth and scaleless. It lives in deep, slow-flowing waters of the middle and lower reaches of large rivers. In the daytime it stays close to the water surface and feeds on insects which have fallen onto it. It also often leaps out of the water. It spawns in May on water plants and its fry live on plankton. The bleak provides an important component in the food chain for predatory fish, whilst its scales are used for the manufacture of artificial mother-of-pearl.

It inhabits an area stretching north from the Pyrenees and the Alps across the whole of Europe as far as the Urals. However, it is not found in Ireland, Wales, Scotland, northern Scandinavia, the Iberian and Italian peninsulas or in Dalmatia.

The schneider differs from the bleak in that it has a higher body and a double dark stripe, which highlights the lateral line at the front of its body. Along with the minnow, it lives in shallow waters in the upper reaches of rivers. It prefers middle layers of water, spawns in May and June and feeds on insects and their larvae. It lives in an area stretching from France to the Caspian Sea, but cannot be found south of the Alps and the Pyrenees, nor in Denmark, northern Europe or in the British Isles.

Alburnus alburnus
Maximum size and weight:
17 cm, 80 g.
Identifying characteristics:
Distinctive mouth strongly oblique. Large, loose, silvery scales; belly behind ventral fins forms a scaleless keel.

Alburnoides bipunctatus
Maximum size and weight:
15 cm, 60 g.
Identifying characteristics:
A double dark stripe on sides, edging lateral line in front of body. Body deeper than that of the bleak.

1 – *Alburnus alburnus*,
2 – *Alburnoides bipunctatus*

1

2

Silver Bream

Cyprinidae

Blicca bjoerkna

The silver bream has a very deep body, which is flattened at the sides; the mouth is in a semi-inferior position and the eyes are relatively large. Its back is scaleless towards the front of its body, as is also its keel behind the pelvic fins. Older specimens have dark, grey-green back, silvery sides and a white belly. The fin edges are grey and the bases of the pectoral and pelvic fins are red or orange. Occasionally the silver bream reaches a length of 35 cm.

It is a generally prolific inhabitant of the river bed in the lower reaches of large rivers, in old river backwaters and pools, in creeks and even in some lowland ponds. It spawns from the end of April to June on aquatic plants. Its food consists of planktonic organisms, algae and the larvae of water insects.

It is found in Europe to the north of the Alps and the Pyrenees as far as southern Scandinavia. It also inhabits the eastern parts of England and the northern Danubian tributaries of the Black Sea.

It crossbreeds in some localities with other fish such as the bream and the roach, but these hybrids are sterile. Economically it is relatively unimportant and is only caught in large quantities in a few rivers and ponds. In terms of fishery management it represents an undesirable fish species, as it sometimes multiplies excessively, although it grows relatively slowly.

Maximum size and weight: 35 cm, 1 kg. *Identifying characteristics:* A high, laterally flattened body; eyes relatively large. Sides strikingly silvery and bases of paired fins reddish.

1 – adult fish,
2 – young fish

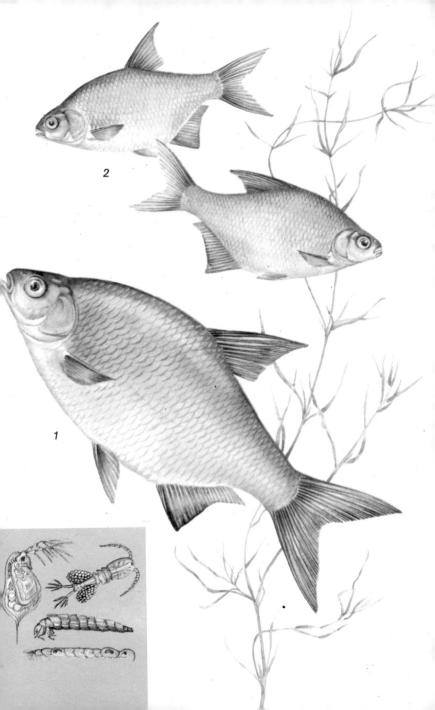

2

1

Common Bream

Cyprinidae

Abramis brama

The common bream is a prolific fish living in great numbers in the lower reaches of slow-flowing, large rivers, lowland reservoirs and lakes. It has a high, laterally flattened body with lead-blue back and silvery or sometimes, in older fish, golden sides. Its eyes are quite small and its fins are a dark to dirty grey; the paired fins are lighter in colour. It is a typical representative of river-bed fish, fond of undergrowths of water vegetation. It even survives in brackish waters, but such types migrate to spawn in clear river waters. Spawning takes place mainly in the evening and during the night towards the end of April and in May on submerged aquatic plants or other suitable objects, such as the foliage of fallen trees. During this period the common bream congregates in large shoals close to the river banks and the males have conspicuous spawning tubercles covering their body and head. Its mouth can be protruded forward during the search for food along the soft river bed. The common bream when young feeds on planktonic animals, but as it becomes larger feeds on benthic organisms. It usually grows to a length of 30 cm and on rare occasions even reaches 75 cm and a weight of over 6 kg.

It inhabits the whole of Europe to the north of the Pyrenees and the Alps, but does not exist in the western and southern parts of the Balkan peninsula or in the western and northern regions of Scandinavia. Its subspecies *Abramis brama orientalis* lives in the watershed of the Caspian Sea and another subspecies, *Abramis brama danubii*, has been found in the mouth of the Danube.

Maximum size and weight: 75 cm, 11 kg. *Identifying characteristics:* A deep, laterally flattened body, with silvery or golden sides. Fins dark, dirty grey. Eyes relatively small. Mouth protrusible.

1 – adult fish,
2 – detail of head with spawning tubercles,
3 – fish collecting food

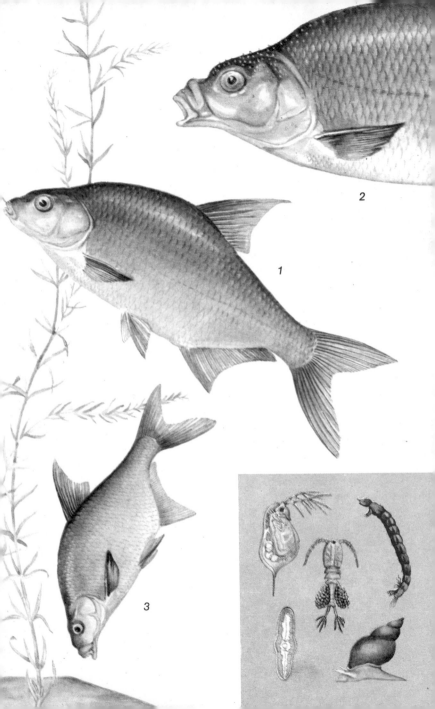

1

2

3

Danube Bream

Abramis sapa

Zope

Abramis ballerus

The Danube bream is a relatively long but deep-bodied fish, appreciably flattened at the sides, and with a long anal fin. Its mouth is in a just ventral position and the snout is blunt. The back is grey-blue or greenish, whilst the sides are silvery. Both migratory and non-migratory populations have been identified, both of which spawn in April and May on aquatic plants growing on the river bed. It feeds mainly on small bottom-living animals, such as insect larvae and small molluscs, and to some extent on vegetation.

It inhabits the tributaries of the Black, Caspian and Azov Seas and the River Danube. The migratory populations swim to the sea after spawning.

The zope is similar in appearance to the Danube bream, except that it has an oblique terminal mouth. It has a dark blue or greenish back and silvery white sides. Its fins are grey, but the pectoral and pelvic fins are yellowish and darker towards the edges. It lives in small shoals in rivers and lakes and its main diet consists of plankton, especially cyclops. It spawns in April and May on water plants.

It lives in the lakes and lower reaches of rivers around the eastern North Sea and Baltic Sea, namely between the Elbe and Neva, the rivers of southern Sweden and Finland and the hinterland of the Black Sea from the Danube to the River Ural. It even penetrates into the Danube as far as upper Austria.

Abramis sapa
Maximum size and weight:
30 cm, 800 g.
Identifying characteristics:
Long anal fin and nearly ventral mouth. Snout blunt and rounded. Fins grey, pectoral and pelvic fins yellowish.

Abramis ballerus
Maximum size and weight:
45 cm, 1.5 kg.
Identifying characteristics:
Long anal fin, mouth terminal, tilted upwards. Fins grey, pectoral and pelvic fins yellowish, darker along edges.

1 – *Abramis sapa*,
2 – *Abramis ballerus*

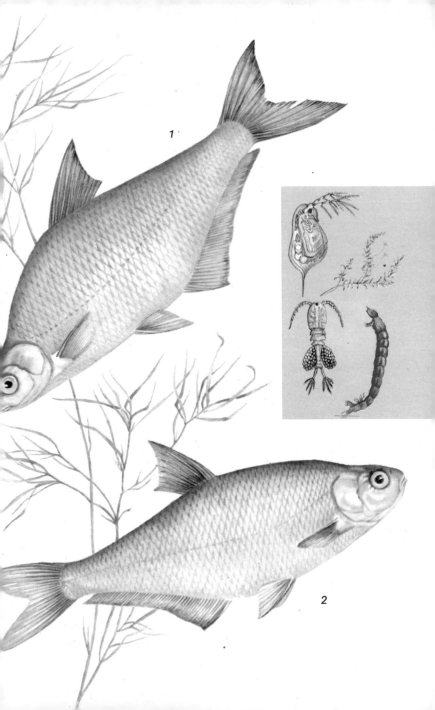

1

2

Zahrte

Vimba vimba

Cyprinidae

The zahrte has a long body and an inferior mouth lying below a fleshy snout. Its belly behind the pelvic fins has a scaleless keel. The back is blue-grey and the belly a clear white. In the breeding season its colouring becomes darker and the front part of its body along with its paired fins turn bright orange. The zahrte is a semi-migratory fish, inhabiting the lower reaches of large, slow-flowing rivers. It can also be found in lakes, where it often has a local economic importance. It spawns in May and June on a stony bed against strong current. Its food consists mainly of bottom-living invertebrates. It reaches a length of 30 to 40 cm and a weight in excess of 1 kg.

This fish is commonly found in the Weser, Elbe and other eastern European rivers as far as the Neva. It also lives in southern Finland and Sweden and has a number of geographically differentiated forms, of which *Vimba vimba carinata* lives in the Danube and *Vimba vimba melanops* in the rivers of southern Bulgaria and the lakes of northern Austria. Its economic importance is negligible as it can only be caught in large numbers in few rivers and lakes.

Maximum size and weight: 40 cm, 2 kg. *Identifying characteristics:* Inferior mouth and fleshy, overlapping snout. Scaleless keel starts behind pelvic fin.

1 – adult fish,
2 – detail of head,
3 – young fish

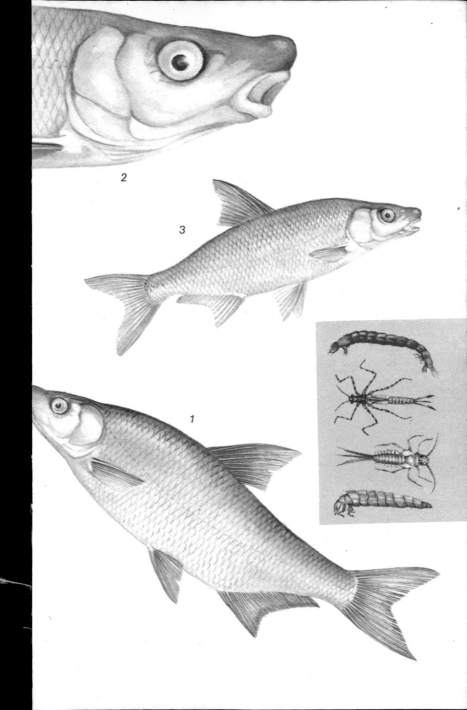

Ziege

Cyprinidae

Pelecus cultratus

The ziege inhabits the top layers of the brackish waters of the Baltic, Black, Aral and Caspian Seas. Its body is relatively long and laterally compressed and it has a wavy lateral line. Its pectoral fins are unusually long and its mouth is steeply oblique. Its dorsal fin is very narrow and deep, whilst its body scales are easily detached and in this respect it is similar to the bleak. Between May and July it migrates from the sea to spawn in rivers, where depending on the salinity its eggs may float. In exceptional circumstances it reaches a length of 60 cm and a weight of 2 kg, its usual size is only 30 cm and 0.5 kg. In the daytime it remains close to the bottom, only rising to the surface in the evening. Young ziege live on plankton, but at a relatively early age also start to feed on small fish and insects which have fallen into the water.

It is quite prolific in the Danube as far as Bratislava and in the lower reaches of such tributaries as the Nitra, Bodrog, and Latorica.

Maximum size and weight: 60 cm, 2 kg. *Identifying characteristics:* Long, laterally flattened body, steeply angled mouth and jagged lateral line. Pectoral fins very long.

1 – adult fish,
2 – detail of head,
3 – view from below

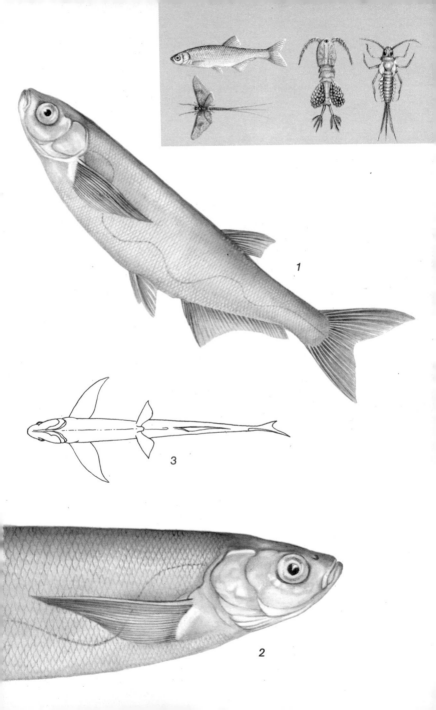

Crucian Carp

Carassius carassius

The crucian carp at first sight looks like the carp, but differs from it in the absence of barbels at the corners of its mouth. Its basic colouring is golden or a dirty green with darker colours predominating on the back and turning to yellow on the sides. The dorsal and caudal fins are brown, whilst the paired fins are yellow-brown or often reddish. The unbranched spiny ray in the dorsal fin has a dense serration of fine teeth. The crucian carp reaches a length of 40 cm and a weight of over 1 kg. Usually it lives in old waterways and pools in the lower reaches of rivers or in swamps and hollows. It stays close to the bottom, where it feeds on small invertebrates. It can withstand low oxygen levels and sometimes hibernates in places which lack oxygen completely. It spawns in May and June on aquatic vegetation.

The most inappropriate places are frequented by a dwarf form (the *humilis* form) of the crucian carp, which grows very slowly and is characterized by a lower body than that of the well fed crucian carp. This dwarf form has a dark spot on its caudal peduncle, which only characterizes young specimens of the crucian carp.

The crucian carp lives in an area stretching from England across to north-eastern France and to the river systems opening into the North and Baltic Seas. Formerly it was also artificially reared in carp ponds.

Maximum size and weight:
40 cm, 1 kg.
Identifying characteristics:
No barbels around mouth. Body cavity coloured light internally, without pigmentation. Long spine in dorsal fin densely serrated with fine teeth.

1 – *Carassius carassius,*
2 – *Carassius carassius* m. *humilis*

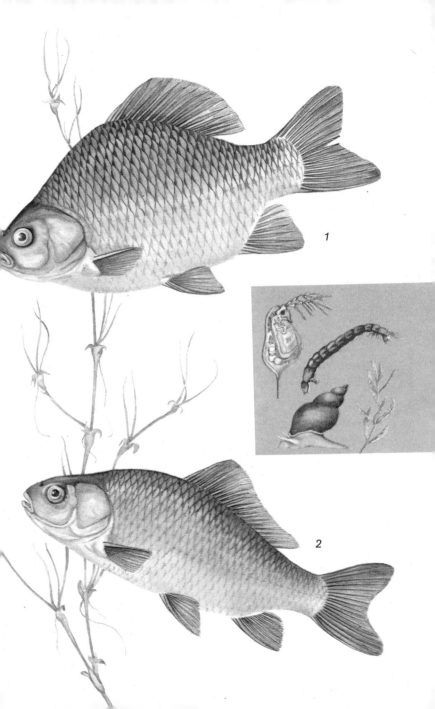

1

2

The Goldfish or Gibel Carp

Carassius auratus gibelio

Cyprinidae

The goldfish is similar in appearance to the crucian carp, but has only a few relatively large teeth on the long spiny ray of the dorsal fin and also has black-pigmented body tissue in the ventral cavity. Additionally, its colouring is slightly different as it has a black-grey back and silvery, sometimes also dark or golden sides. The dorsal and caudal fins are black-grey, whilst the paired fins and the anal fin are much lighter. It lives together with the crucian carp and spawns between May and July. The goldfish living on the boundaries of its habitat are characterized by the following phenomena: in such places only females can usually be found, and their eggs are fertilized by other members of the carp family, especially by the carp and the crucian carp. The offspring are generally females again, and are genetically identical with the goldfish parent. The diet of the goldfish has the usual animal component with the addition of large quantities of aquatic vegetation.

Originally it came from eastern Asia and Siberia but today is distributed throughout eastern, central and northern Europe and continues to spread westwards. The exact boundaries to its range are not as yet known because of the difficulties of distinguishing it from the crucian carp. Finally the goldfish which is so common in ponds and aquaria is simply a selectively bred variety of a subspecies found in China, Korea and Japan.

Maximum size and weight: 35 cm, 1.2 kg. *Identifying characteristics:* Black-pigmented body tissue in ventral cavity; spiny fin ray of dorsal fin with a small number of medium-size teeth (10—15).

1 – *Carassius auratus gibelio*, 2 – *Carassius auratus auratus*

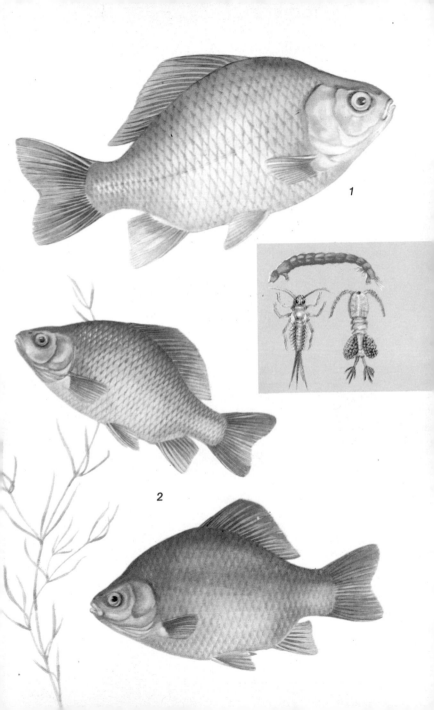

1

2

Carp

Cyprinus carpio

The domesticated carp displays a number of variations in the nature of the scale covering of its body. The most common pond variety is the mirror carp, whose body is irregularly covered with scales of different sizes. Another variety has a row of scales along the sides of the body and sometimes a similar line of scales on the base of the dorsal fin, whilst the leather carp either has no scales at all or only a few individual scales below the dorsal fin and along the base of other fins.

The carp is a most valuable fish, which is readily appreciated also by anglers, on whose behalf it is stocked in open waters. The ponds used for carp breeding are looked after in the same way as fields or other agricultural areas. The rapid development of large quantities of fish food, which will ensure the fast growth of the carp, is achieved by letting the water out of such ponds in summer, by cutting back undesirable growths of vegetation, by fertilizing the land with organic and inorganic fertilizers and by chemically improving the quality of the water when the pond is refilled.

Carp are introduced to rivers and valley reservoirs either as fry when they weigh a mere 30 to 50 g or when they are a year old and weigh 200 to 500 g.

Maximum size and weight: 120 cm, 30 kg. *Identifying characteristics:* Large scales, long dorsal and short anal fins. Mouth has four fleshy barbels.

1 – wild form from the Danube, 2 – view from above, 3 – scale

1

2

3

Carp

Cyprinus carpio

The original home of the carp is the watershed of the Black and Caspian Seas, but as it has become a most popular pond fish, it has slowly been dispersed all over Europe. During the past century it has also been introduced to the United States, as well as parts of Africa, Australia, and New Zealand. In the warmer parts of the USA it has multiplied exceedingly, often to the detriment of native fishes and aquatic vegetation. It can be as much as 120 cm long and can weigh over 30 kg. It has large scales, a long dorsal and a short anal fin. At the corners of the mouth it has four barbels. The original wild form of the carp *(Cyprinus carpio)* has a long, cylindrical, scaly body. This lives in the Danube and some of its tributaries. Spawning takes place between May and June and the spawn sticks to water plants or to the flooded grass of the river banks. The fry lives on zooplankton and when 2 cm long, progresses to a diet of bottom-living invertebrates, whilst in thickly overgrown waters the carp also lives on water plants. In Europe it is by far the most commercially important freshwater fish and a number of varieties of carp are pond-bred and then transplanted to rivers, reservoirs and warm lakes. The carp easily crossbreeds with the crucian carp and such hybrids have two pairs of very short barbels, grow more slowly than the carp and are usually sterile.

In recent decades, the wild form of the carp has been used in crossbreeding experiments with the cultivated forms. Such hybrids are more resistant to various infectious diseases and grow very well indeed.

Maximum size and weight: 120 cm, 30 kg. *Identifying characteristics:* Large scales, long dorsal and short anal fins. Mouth has four fleshy barbels.

1 – pond form called 'spiegel', 2 – scale

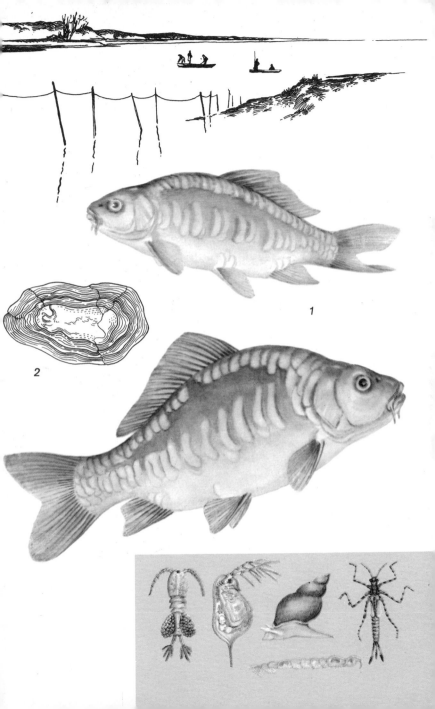

1

2

Carp

Cyprinus carpio

Carp breeding in ponds is a very old tradition in Europe. It requires a series of ponds each serving a different purpose. For example breeding ponds are usually small artificial pools often overgrown with grass, which house female fish during the spawning period. After spawning the mother fish are removed and when the larvae have absorbed the egg yolk, they are taken out by fine nets and transferred to fry ponds. There they stay until autumn, when they are again transferred to deep ponds, to overwinter. In spring the carp are transplanted yet again to another type of growing pond and in the autumn of the second year, when the carp weighs 200 to 500 g, it is relocated in deeper ponds. In the third year the young are put into the large, main ponds, in which by autumn they have reached the correct size for consumption, namely 1.5 to 3 kg. During this process the carp is given extra food, which includes natural food-stuffs, such as peas and grain, as well as special feed additives. Female carp which weigh about 5 to 10 kg and have the desired features, are then used for breeding purposes. In this way the breeding stock is kept pure in the carp-farm.

Maximum size and weight: 120 cm, 30 kg. *Identifying characteristics:* Large scales, long dorsal and short anal fins. Mouth has four fleshy barbels.

1 – pond form with scales,
2 – alevins

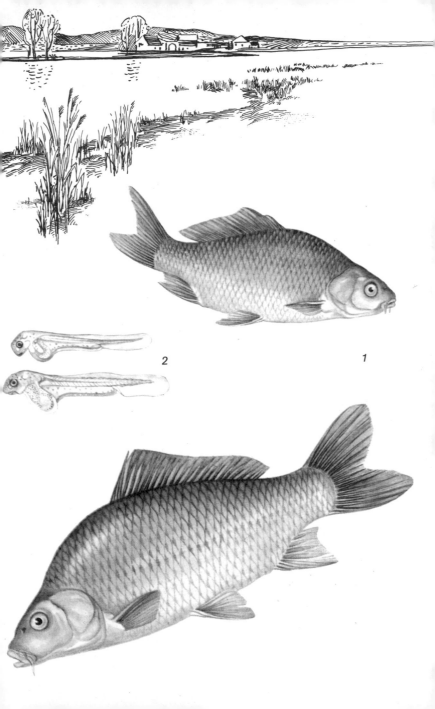

1

2

Carp

Cyprinus carpio

The care of carp ponds resembles in many respects common agricultural practice used in the management of arable fields and pastures. Such ponds are from time to time left dry and fallow in summer or in winter. In summer the pond bed is ploughed up, fertilized and used for the cultivation of various specialized plants, such as clover and lucerne. These areas are then often flooded in the autumn and the plants in decaying enrich the water.

Throughout the carp breeders' aim is to achieve the highest possible fish production. Thus by appropriate fertilization they increase the amount of small water organisms, which then become the carp food. From time to time the ponds are cultivated with the assistance of heavy machinery, which breaks up the hard, overgrown edges and increases the productive area of the pond. In summer also the fishermen cut down rushes and other offshore vegetation by using special purpose-built boats. In winter a range of machinery is installed in the ponds to prevent the formation of ice and to guarantee a continuous supply of oxygen in the water. During the autumn fish harvest, the pond managers first of all let the water out and at the same time prevent the fish from escaping by constructing a compact fencing near the water outlet. Then the carp, which have become concentrated in the deepest part of the pond, are caught in nets. The fish are then sorted, placed in wooden tanks and transported by lorries to storage tanks.

Maximum size and weight: 120 cm, 30 kg. *Identifying characteristics:* Large scales, long dorsal and short anal fins. Mouth has four fleshy barbels.

1 – pond scaleless form, 2 – crustacean parasite *Argulus*, 3 – wind defreezer

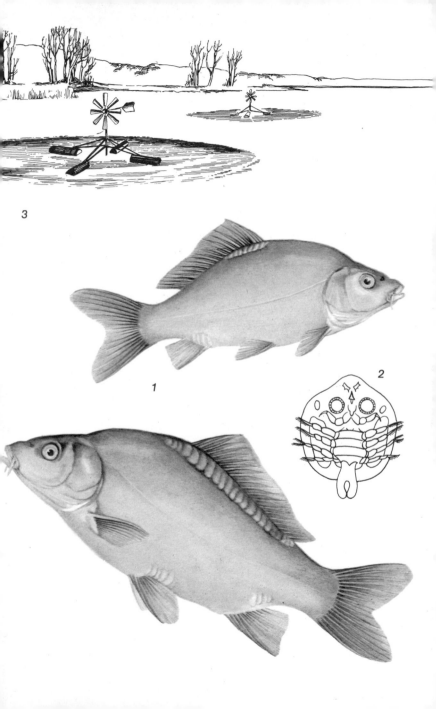

3

1

2

Silver Carp

Cyprinidae

Hypophthalmichthys molitrix

Grass Carp

Ctenopharyngodon idella

The silver carp has its eyes in an unusually low position on the head. Its belly from its throat to the anal opening has a sharp, scaleless keel. Its eggs are pelagic and are carried by the current. The adult fish feed almost exclusively on plant plankton and grow very quickly.

It inhabits the vast area of eastern Asia stretching from the River Amur in the USSR as far as the rivers of the Canton province in southern China. In China this fish has been bred in ponds for a long time. In recent years it has been acclimatized even in Europe, where it sometimes escapes from ponds to open waters, such as the Danube.

The grass carp has a long, scaly body, which is slightly flattened at the sides. Its head is very wide and the mouth is in a semi-inferior position. In colouring it resembles the carp, but its sides are somewhat lighter and have a golden sheen. All its fins are dark grey and there are conspicuous ridges on its gill covers. This species often grows to more than 1 m in length and weighs up to 32 kg. It spawns in spring and its eggs are pelagic. It feeds predominantly on vegetation. In ponds it is given a supplementary diet of clover and lucerne.

Originally it came from the middle and lower reaches of the River Amur and its tributaries. In China it is bred in ponds to the south of Canton, and several decades ago it was also acclimatized for the first time in the European part of the USSR and in some other European countries. Experimentally, it has been introduced to England and the United States; in both it has been released to help control growths of aquatic plants.

Hypophthalmichthys molitrix
Maximum size and weight:
1 m, 10 kg.
Identifying characteristics:
Belly forms sharp, scaleless keel, extending from throat to anus. Eyes located very low on head, mouth tilts upwards. Protrusion in lower jaw slots into hollow in upper jaw.

Ctenopharyngodon idella
Maximum size and weight:
130 cm, 32 kg.
Identifying characteristics:
Large terminal mouth and elongated, cylindrical body. Gills have conspicuous radial dents.

1 – *Hypophthalmichthys molitrix*,
2 – *Ctenopharyngodon idella*

1

2

Weatherfish

Misgurnus fossilis

Stone Loach

Noemacheilus barbatulus

The weatherfish is a long-bodied fish with the body compressed at the sides and with ten barbels at the sides of its mouth. It lives in muddy, stagnant waters, in river backwaters and also in ponds. In any sudden change of air pressure it will swim close to the water surface and move about briskly. If oxygen is sparse in the water, it will gulp in air and absorb the oxygen through the mucous membrane of its gut. It spawns in May and the embryos have special external, web-like gills which soon disappear. In Europe it can be found from the Seine to the Neva and from the Danube to the Volga. However, it does not live in rivers flowing into the Arctic Ocean or in rivers in England, Scandinavia, Finland and southern Europe.

The stone loach is a small, 10 to 18 cm long fish with a cylindrical, dark-marbled body and with six barbels at the mouth. The back is greenish or brownish, the sides are yellowish with irregular black-brown spots. The belly is whitish grey, sometimes with a pinkish tint. The fish keeps close to the bottom in rivers as well as in ponds and lakes, and usually hides under stones and roots. It spawns in spring during the month of May on sandy or stony shallows. Its diet consists chiefly of the larvae of water insects, such as the red midge. It is most active at night or in the half-light. It occurs all over Europe with the exception of northern Scotland, northern Scandinavia, southern and central Italy and Greece.

Misgurnus fossilis
Maximum size and weight:
35 cm, 150 g.
Identifying characteristics:
Long body, compressed on the sides. Ten barbels at the mouth. Lateral longitudinal stripes.

Noemacheilus barbatulus
Maximum size and weight:
18 cm, 80 g.
Identifying characteristics:
Elongated, cylindrical body with dark marbling. Six barbels at the mouth. Scales very small.

1 – *Misgurnus fossilis,*
1a – larva,
2, 3, – *Noemacheilus barbatulus*

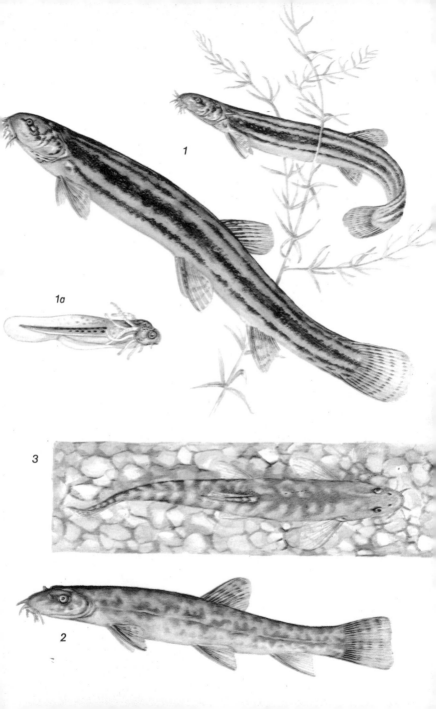

1
1a
3
2

Spined Loach
Cobitis taenia

Sabanajewia aurata reaches a length of 10 cm at the most and has a slender and very compressed body. It has six barbels at its mouth and a characteristic sharp spine below its eyes, which can be erected. There are 8 to 15 square spots on its sides. Its caudal peduncle has a leathery keel. It lives amongst stones and gravel in deep currents in the middle and lower reaches of rivers. It spawns in April and May and feeds on bottom-living animals.

It occurs in northern Iran and the adjacent part of the USSR, in Anatolia and the watershed of the River Don, in the basin of the Danube and in the Balkans. It has a number of geographical races. This fish is placed in the genus *Cobitis* by many scientists.

The spined loach grows to about 6 or 7 cm, rarely 10 cm, in length. It has a slim, elongated and very compressed body and head. Its inferior-positioned mouth has six barbels. A sharp, erectile double spine is placed beneath each eye. It has 14 to 16 small dark blotches on its sides and a conspicuous one on the top side of its caudal fin. It lives close to the bottom in stagnant and slow-flowing waters and likes to bury itself in the silt. It spawns in April and May and feeds on aquatic invertebrates.

It is distributed all over Europe with the exception of Norway, northern Sweden, Finland, the USSR, Scotland and Greece. In Europe there exist a number of geographical races.

Sabanajewia aurata
Maximum size and weight:
10 cm, 5 g.
Identifying characteristics:
Long, compressed body and head, 6 barbels at the mouth, 8—14 large, square, dark spots on sides and leathery keel between dorsal and caudal fins.

Cobitis taenia
Maximum size and weight:
10 cm, 5 g.
Identifying characteristics:
Long, compressed body and head, 6 barbels at the mouth, 14—16 dark spots on sides and conspicuous dark fleck on top of caudal fin.

1 – *Sabanajewia aurata*,
2 – *Cobitis taenia*

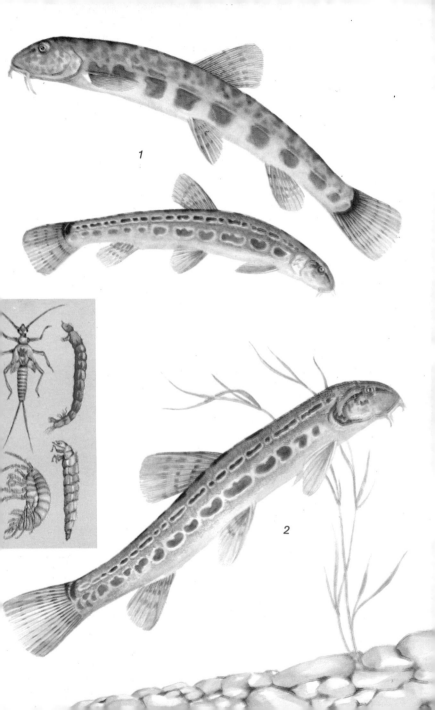

Wels or European Catfish

Silurus glanis

The wels is a large fish with a long, scaleless body, a very small dorsal and a rounded caudal fin, which touches the long anal fin. Its mouth is equipped with three pairs of barbels; the one located on the upper jaw is very long. The back is plain, either olive-green or blue-grey, but the sides often have a marble-like pattern. The wels lives close to the bottom in the deep waters of large rivers, reservoirs and lakes. It spawns from May to July in the shallows, where the female constructs a kind of nest. After mating the male guards the spawn and later the fry. During the day the wels usually hides close to the bottom, but is active at night, when it seeks its food on the water surface. It feeds on various types of small fish, small mammals and water birds. It grows very quickly and in Europe achieves a length of about 2 m and a weight of over 50 kg, although in some regions, for example in the Danube basin, it grows still much larger. Young wels often live in schools and only become solitary when adult.

In Europe it can be found to the east of the upper reaches of the River Rhine, in the River Elbe and in rivers flowing into the Baltic Sea and in the tributaries of the Black and Caspian Seas; it is localized in Sweden, and has been introduced to England. Its relative, *Silurus aristotelis*, lives in Greece.

Maximum size and weight: 3 m, 300 kg. *Identifying characteristics:* Scaleless body with small dorsal fin; rounded caudal fin touches anal fin. Three pairs of barbels; pair on upper jaw very long. Mouth wide, head depressed from above.

1 – adult fish,
2 – alevin,
3 – detail of head

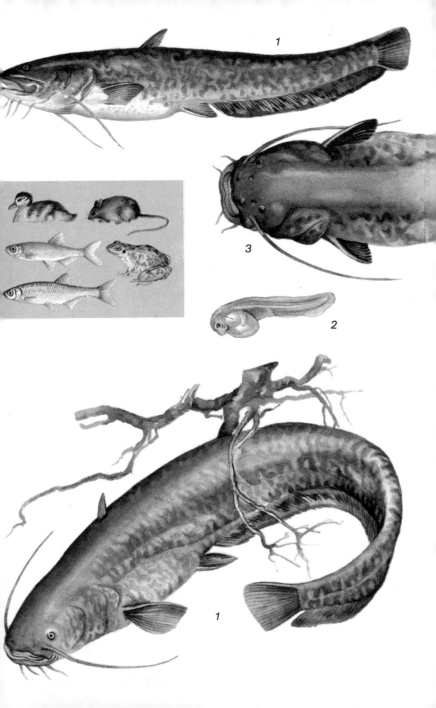

Brown Bullhead

Ictalurus nebulosus

The brown bullhead is a North American species which was imported into Europe at the turn of this century and has since multiplied profusely in many suitable rivers. It has similarities with the wels, but has a fleshy adipose fin between its dorsal and caudal fins, whilst its mouth is equipped with eight long barbels. Its back is brown-green to black, the lighter sides have a golden sheen and the white belly turns yellow to orange-yellow during the mating season. Its dorsal and pectoral fins contain a strong, thorny ray. It spawns from April to June, when the female lays her cream-coloured eggs in a bowl-shaped nest and the males subsequently guard them and later also the young fry. After the spawning season large shoals of dark-coloured, young brown bullheads can be seen swimming close to the water surface. This species can endure low oxygen levels in water, and like the crucian carp or the weatherfish it can survive in waters where other fish would suffocate. It is omnivorous, as it consumes both vegetable and animal food, and in Europe grows to a length of about 25 to 30 cm and a weight of about 0.5 kg.

It is a native inhabitant of southern Canada and the USA and is abundant in the large North American lakes and the watershed of the St. Lawrence river.

A second and similar American catfish, the black bullhead *(I. melas)*, has also been introduced to Europe.

Maximum size and weight: 30 cm, 500 g. *Identifying characteristics:* Resembles the wels, but has an adipose fin on the back and 8 long barbels at the wide mouth. Strong spines in its dorsal and pectoral fins.

1 – adult fish,
2 – alevin,
3 – belly

European Eel

Anguilla anguilla

The European eel has a long, snake-like body without pelvic fins. It has small scales, which are deeply embedded in the skin so much so as to be virtually invisible. Its extremely long dorsal and anal fins merge with the caudal fin and thus form a continuous edging to the whole of its body. It spawns in the Atlantic Ocean in the region of the Sargasso Sea, east of the Bermudas and Bahamas. The larvae differ considerably from the adult fish as they look like transparent willow leaves. For about three years they are slowly carried by the Gulf Stream towards the European continent, where they change into minute, snake-like elvers. Young eels have dark green or brown-black backs and their bellies and sides are yellowish or white. The females then travel upriver, while the males remain in the river estuaries. At the start of their breeding migration the adult fish have large eyes, shiny, metal-coloured sides and a silvery white belly. The females live in freshwater for twelve years or more and then return to the Atlantic Ocean, where after spawning they are believed to die.

The European eel lives close to the river bed under roots and in other hideouts, only becoming active at night. Many travel short distances overland (usually on wet nights) to get to isolated ponds. They are usually 100 to 150 cm long and weigh up to 4 kg, although in exceptional cases they grow to 2 m in length and achieve a weight of 7 kg.

Maximum size and weight: 2 m, 7 kg. *Identifying characteristics:* Snake-like body; no pelvic fins. Dorsal, caudal and anal fins form a continuous fin edging. Minute scales deeply embedded in skin.

1 – adult fish,
2 – development,
3a – broad-headed form,
3b – narrow-headed form,
4 – spawning grounds in the Atlantic

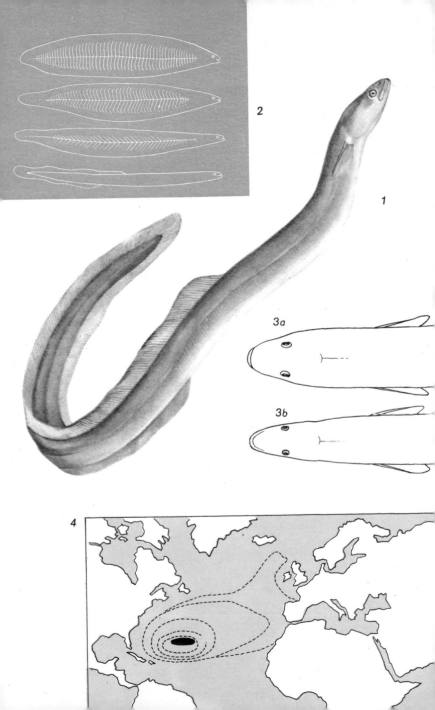

1

2

3a

3b

4

Golden Grey Mullet
Liza aurata

Common Grey Mullet
Mugil cephalus

The golden grey mullet can reach a length of 50 cm, is slightly compressed at the sides and has a very depressed head and a wide mouth, which does not extend back to reach the eyes. It has large scales and an indistinct lateral line. Its two short dorsal fins are well apart, and the first of these consists of only 4 strong spines. The back is brownish and the sides have 6 to 7 dark brown longitudinal stripes. The belly is white and there is a golden spot behind the eye and another on the gill cover. It feeds on minute organisms living in the bottom mud. It lives in small shoals in the sea and likes to migrate far upriver. Often can it be found in the lower reaches of rivers stretching from the North Sea along the entire European coastline round to the Mediterranean and Black Seas.

The common grey mullet reaches a length of 70 cm. Its back is greyish with a golden and blue metallic sheen; its sides have 9 to 10 dark longitudinal stripes and the gill covers have a golden and silvery sheen. Its biology generally resembles that of the previous species. It can be found hugging the shores of the Indian, Pacific and Atlantic Oceans and in Europe from the estuary of the river Loire southwards. All the grey mullet species have a considerable economic value, for their flesh is very tasty and thus they are usually caught in various types of nets.

Liza aurata
Maximum size and weight:
50 cm, 2 kg.
Identifying characteristics:
Two short dorsal fins; first has only 4 strong, spiky rays.
6—7 dark brown longitudinal stripes on the sides and golden spots on gill covers and behind eyes.

Mugil cephalus
Maximum size and weight:
70 cm, 4 kg.
Identifying characteristics:
Two short dorsal fins; first has only 4 strong, spiky rays.
9—10 dark longitudinal stripes on the sides; gill covers have golden and silvery sheen.

1 – *Liza aurata*,
1a – view from above,
2 – *Mugil cephalus*
2a – view from above

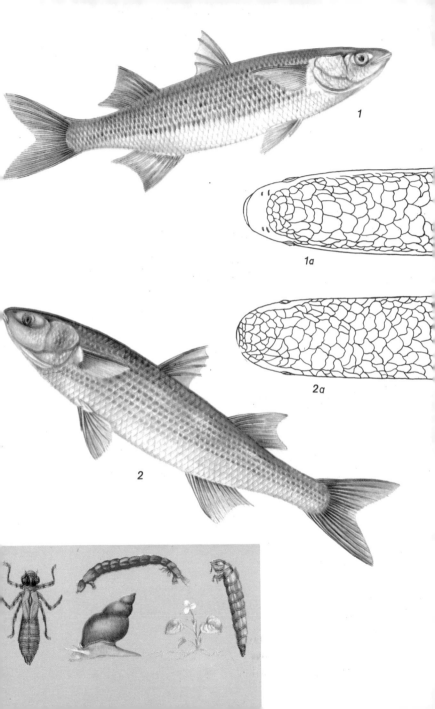

1

1a

2

2a

Perch

Perca fluviatilis

The perch is one of the most abundant of European fish and is characterized by its oblong body, which is flattened at the sides and has two dorsal fins (the first strongly spiny) and ctenoid scales. The top half of the body is a dark grey to blue or olive green, the belly is lighter. It has 6 to 9 dark transverse stripes on its sides. On the back edge of the first dorsal fin there is a black spot, whilst the pelvic and anal fins are red. It grows to a length of 30 to 50 cm and averages a weight of 1 to 2 kg, although in exceptional conditions this rises up to 5 kg. It lives in both flowing and stagnant waters, but especially likes to linger in creeks close to banks overgrown with water vegetation in the middle and lower river reaches, in old water ways, in ponds, lakes and lowland reservoirs. It usually remains near the river bed and spawns between April and May. Its eggs are laid and fertilized in long strips which are wrapped round the remains of water plants and submerged tree branches. These strips of spawn are often 1 to 2 m long and 1 to 2 cm wide.

Young perch usually form small schools, but older fish are much more isolated and independent. Perch living in enclosed waters frequently overmultiply to such an extent that they squeeze out other fish species and they themselves become stunted individually. They feed on aquatic invertebrates and small fishes, although older and larger perch live exclusively on fish.

It is found all over Europe with the exception of Scotland, the Iberian peninsula, Italy, the western Balkans, the Crimea and northern Norway. It is closely related to the North American yellow perch *(Perca flavescens)*.

Maximum size and weight: 60 cm, 5 kg. *Identifying characteristics:* A black spot at end of first dorsal fin and 6—9 dark transverse stripes on sides. Pelvic and anal fins reddish.

adult fish

Zander or Pikeperch

Stizostedion lucioperca

Percidae

The zander is a sturdy fish which grows over 1 m in length and often weighs up to 12 kg. It has a long body and a pointed, slightly depressed head. The mouth is large and extends back to the front edge of the eye. The jaws contain many small teeth, interspersed with impressive, projecting larger teeth. The back of the zander is a dark olive green, the sides are lighter, whilst the belly is white or silvery. It has eight or more dark transverse stripes on the sides. The zander lives close to the bottom in the deeper parts of the middle and lower reaches of rivers with sandy or muddy bottoms. Usually it swims to the surface only in the morning or evening when it is hunting for fish. It is often artificially reared in ponds and then put in dampools, lakes and rivers. It spawns in April and May in the shallows, where it constructs a nest which has a diameter of about 0.5 m. These nests contain plant roots to which the eggs are fastened. The male guards the eggs and fans clean water over them. In Europe the zander lives to the east of the watersheds of the rivers Rhine and Danube, although in recent years it has been introduced into many other areas including eastern England. It is an important fish with excellent flesh and is therefore caught in various types of nets and also highly prized by anglers.

It is closely related to the North American walleye, also a much valued angling fish.

Maximum size and weight: 130 cm, 12 kg. *Identifying characteristics:* Elongated cylindrical body; blackish-brown stripes on the sides often disintegrate into individual spots. Large 'canine' teeth in front parts of the jaws.

1 – adult fish,
2 – detail of head

1

2

Eastern Pikeperch or Eastern Zander

Stizostedion volgense

The Eastern pikeperch is very similar to the zander, but is generally smaller and its first dorsal fin is very high. Its jaws do not contain the strikingly large teeth of the zander and the whole of its front gill cover is covered with scales. It has similar colouring, but its transverse stripes are usually more distinctive and do not disintegrate into a series of spots. It is smaller in size and rarely exceeds a length of 50 cm or a weight of about 2 kg. It inhabits the deeper, sandy or stony stretches of rivers, where it likes to hide in the irregularities of the river bed and under the banks. It spawns in April and May in the shallows and, as with the zander, the male guards the nest. The Eastern pikeperch catches its food, which consists predominantly of fish, mainly in the evening and at night. It feeds even during the coldest season.

It inhabits the tributaries of the Black and Caspian Seas, from the Danube as far as the River Ural. It can easily be mistaken for the zander and therefore it is sometimes mistakenly regarded as being very rare. In fact it lives in large numbers along with the zander in the River Danube (close to Bratislava) and in its backwaters.

Maximum size and weight: 50 cm, 2 kg. *Identifying characteristics:* Smaller than zander; the conspicuous stripes do not disintegrate into series of spots. Strikingly large teeth missing.

adult fish

Schraetzer

Gymnocephalus schraetser

Ruffe or Pope

Gymnocephalus cernua

The schraetzer has a long and relatively low body, a pointed head and sharp spines on the gill covers. It may grow up to 24 cm in length. It has an olive-green back and yellow sides, which have 3 to 4 black, sometimes interrupted longitudinal stripes. The front part of its dorsal fin has dark oval spots arranged in regular rows. It is a relatively rare species, but is more abundant in the deep currents and sandy sections of rivers. It occurs in the Danube and its tributaries from Bavaria down to its estuary.

The ruffe is a smallish fish which averages a length of only 10 to 15 cm. It has a grey-green back decorated by dull, dark spots, and brownish sides. Its gill covers have a strong metallic sheen, the belly is yellow-white and the dorsal and tail fins are profusely covered with small dark dots. The first, spiny dorsal fin is fused completely with the second dorsal fin, which in contrast has branched rays. It thrives in the lower reaches of rivers. Its diet consists of small invertebrates and young fish. It spawns between April and June on the river bed.

It lives in an area stretching from eastern England and north-eastern France throughout the whole of Europe. It does not live in Ireland, Scotland, in northern Norway, on the Iberian peninsula, in Italy and in the western and southern Balkans.

Gymnocephalus schraetser
Maximum size and weight:
25 cm, 150 g.
Identifying characteristics:
Long, slender body with large head. Gill covers with long spines. 3—4 black longitudinal stripes along sides.

Gymnocephalus cernua
Maximum size and weight:
15 cm, 70 g.
Identifying characteristics:
Dorsal fins fused into one. Body compressed at sides, lateral line incomplete. Mouth small, terminal; gill covers with spines.

1 – *Gymnocephalus schraetser,*
2 – *Gymnocephalus cernua*

Zingel

Percidae

Zingel zingel

Streber

Zingel streber

The zingel is a long and slender member of the perch family with a large head and a relatively short caudal peduncle. Its mouth is nearly ventral and its body is a yellow-grey with small dark spots and four dark transverse blotches, which often disintegrate into a series of flecks. It lives close to the bottom in the deep currents of rivers. It is relatively immobile and during the daytime hides in suitable hollows. It spawns in April and May on the gravelly river bed. Its diet consists of invertebrates and small fish. It lives in the Danube and Dniester and their tributaries.

The streber is similar to the zingel, but its caudal peduncle is much longer and narrower. Its body is yellow-brown or grey-brown, with 4 to 5 distinct dark, slanting bars. It usually grows to a length of 12 to 17 cm. It lives in the fast-flowing currents near the river bed and is a predominantly nocturnal fish. It spawns in March and April and during this time its body takes on a metallic green sheen. It feeds on a range of invertebrates and inhabits the rivers Danube, Dniester and the tributaries of these rivers, which flow into the Black Sea. As with the preceding species, it penetrates Austria and Bavaria through the Danube.

Zingel zingel
Maximum size and weight:
50 cm, 500 g.
Identifying characteristics:
Long, slender body with large head and nearly ventral mouth. 4 dark, transverse blotches on sides, often breaking up into spots.

Zingel streber
Maximum size and weight:
17 cm, 170 g.
Identifying characteristics:
Long, slender body and strikingly long caudal peduncle, 4—5 conspicuous dark slanting bars on sides.

1 – *Zingel zingel,*
2 – *Zingel streber*

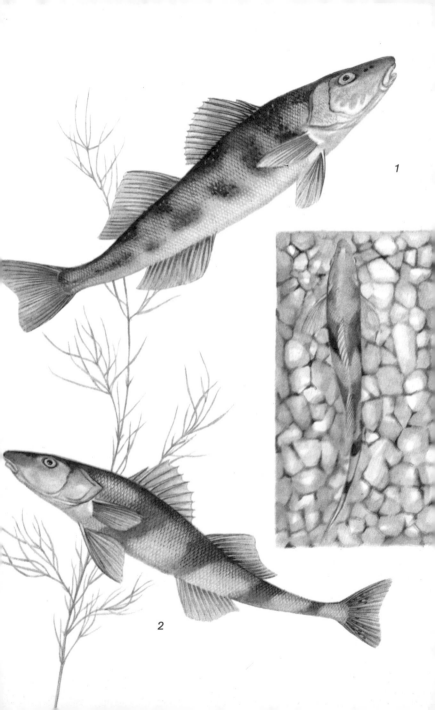

1

2

Bullhead or Miller's Thumb

Cottidae

Cottus gobio

Alpine Bullhead

Cottus poecilopus

The bullhead is a small, rather sedentary fish, with a large head and wide mouth, which inhabits the clean mountain brooks of the trout zone down to small, lowland rivers. Its scaleless body has two dorsal fins. The pelvic fins are whitish and relatively short — they do not extend as far as the anal opening; the inside rays of these fins are over half the length of the longest ray. This fish usually rests under stones and has the advantage that it can adapt perfectly to the colour of its environment. It breeds in April and the male guards the eggs, which are usually stuck to the underside of large stones. It feeds on insect larvae and also is considered (without adequate proof) to be a dangerous predator on trout spawn. It lives throughout Europe from England and the Pyrenees to the Caspian Sea, but it is generally missing in the waters of southern Europe and western and northern regions as Ireland, Scotland, Scandinavia and the north of the USSR.

The Alpine bullhead is similar to the bullhead, although its pelvic fins are differently coloured. They have transverse stripes, are longer and often extend beyond the anal opening. The inside ray of the pelvic fins is short and does not exceed two fifths of the longest ray. It inhabits the watershed of the Arctic Ocean to the east of Scandinavia, also the watershed of the Baltic Sea and the rivers Danube and Dniester. It is generally found at higher altitudes above sea level than the bullhead.

Cottus gobio
Maximum size and weight:
15 cm, 80 g.
Identifying characteristics:
Large head, lateral line complete. Inside ray of pelvic fins more than half the length of longest ray. Pelvic fins white-grey without transverse stripes.

Cottus poecilopus
Maximum size and weight:
15 cm, 80 g.
Identifying characteristics:
Pelvic fins relatively long, extend to anal opening, have transverse stripes. Their inside ray very short, does not reach half the length of the longest ray.

1, 3, 4, – *Cottus gobio,*
2, 5 – *Cottus poecilopus*

Large-mouth Black Bass

Centrarchidae

Micropterus salmoides

This North American fish has been reared in Europe since the 1880s in carp ponds and some Alpine lakes. The spiny part of its dorsal fin is lower than the back portion. It has a long body and a very deeply cleft mouth — the end of the upper jaw extends to the back edge of the eye. Its sides have a wavy black stripe and along with the belly are silvery in colour, whilst the back is dark green. This wavy black stripe is more prominent in younger fish, while in older specimens it is usually much fainter. This fish lives in slow-flowing or stagnant and overgrown waters. In the spawning season, which is May and June, the males guard the eggs and the newly hatched fry. Young large-mouth black bass feed on plankton, but soon also begin to eat the larvae of water insects and when they are older they start habitually catching fish and other small vertebrates, such as frogs.

The native range of this fish is the USA and southern Canada, where it lives in the area of the Great Lakes, in the watershed of the Mississippi and southwards as far as north-eastern Mexico and Florida. In Europe it is usually 35 to 40 cm long and weighs over 2 kg, but in the south of the USA it can weigh as much as 8 kg. It has not been a successful introduction in England.

Maximum size and weight: 45 cm, 2.5 kg. *Identifying characteristics:* Front part of dorsal fin low and spiny, back part higher. Large mouth extends as far as back edge of eye. Wavy black stripe on sides.

adult fish

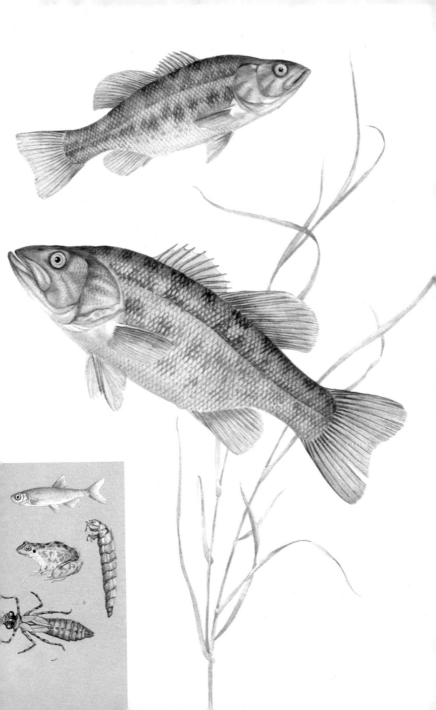

Pumpkinseed
Lepomis gibbosus

The pumpkinseed is a North American fish and a relative of the large-mouth black bass, with which it was also introduced to Europe from the USA. It has an oval, deep body, which is well flattened at the sides, and a small mouth. The front part of the dorsal fin is spiny and longer than the soft-rayed part, to which it is joined. The pectoral fins are long and pointed. The pumpkinseed is very gaily coloured; the back is olive green, the sides are bluish with red or orange circular spots and at the sides of its head there are small blue and orange stripes. The flap of skin at the edge of its gill cover is characterized by black or orange spots. The pumpkinseed is about 15 to 20 cm long and weighs up to 250 g, but average-size fish living in European rivers are much smaller. It inhabits overgrown lakes and river creeks and spawns in May and June, sometimes even later. The eggs are laid in bowl-shaped hollows on the river bed and guarded by the males. They often construct such nests in large colonies. The pumpkinseed's diet consists of plankton, river-bed vertebrates and fish fry.

It is native to North America, particularly an area stretching from Dakota to the Gulf of Mexico. Several related species live in North America. It has been introduced into Europe by aquarists or incidentally along with the fry of more economically important fish. In certain areas, this fish has become too prolific and has forced out other fish species. It occurs in England in two or three isolated localities.

Maximum size and weight: 20 cm, 250 g. *Identifying characteristics:* Spiny portion of dorsal fin is longer than the soft-rayed part. A high body, compressed at sides. Gill protrusions have reddish flecks.

adult fish

Three-spined Stickleback

Gasterosteus aculeatus

The three-spined stickleback is a small fish with a series of 2 to 4 characteristic strong spines forming the front part of the dorsal fin. The pelvic fins are positioned close behind the pectoral fins. The body is spindle-shaped and covered with bony plates. The back is grey-blue, olive-green or grey and the sides are silvery white. It may grow 10 cm long at the most, but the average specimens are about 4 to 6 cm in length. It usually spawns in April, but the breeding season often lasts until June. During this period the colour of the front part of the male's body changes to orange or red, the belly is silvery and the whole body has a distinct metallic sheen. The male, using bits of vegetation, builds a nest into which he drives the female. After spawning he guards the eggs there and for a short time also looks after the fry. Young three-spined sticklebacks feed on small zooplankton, but then progress to larger benthic animals, especially the larvae of the red midge.

This fish is a circumpolar species of the cold and temperate zones of the northern hemisphere. To the north it becomes common in the coastal regions of both the Atlantic and the Pacific. In Europe it lives in an area stretching from the Black Sea, southern Italy and the Iberian peninsula as far as the northern coast of Norway, Newfoundland and Iceland. To the east it inhabits the areas of the watersheds of the rivers Dvina, Dnieper, and as far south as the rivers of the Crimea. It is not found in the watershed of the River Volga or in the southern Balkans. It is widespread in Canada and the United States.

Maximum size and weight: 10 cm, 30 g.
Identifying characteristics: Three isolated spines at front of dorsal fin. Body covered with bony plates.

1 – adult fish ♀,
2 – adult fish ♂

♀

1

♀

1

2

♂

Burbot

Lota lota

The burbot is the only freshwater representative of the cod family. It has a long body, which is compressed at the sides towards the rear. The pelvic fins are located in front of the pectoral pair and their second ray has a thread-like protrusion. The centre of the chin is distinguished by a single barbel. The burbot has two dorsal fins, of which the second is very long, as is also its anal fin. The belly is whitish; the back and sides are grey-brown, the body and fins have a striking, marble-like pattern. It rarely reaches a length of over 1 m or a weight of over 20 kg. The burbot hides close to the river bed or under overhanging banks in the trout, grayling and barbel zones of European rivers, although it is sometimes found in their lower reaches and in lakes or ponds. It is a predatory fish, which feeds predominantly on fish, frogs and other larger vertebrates. It spawns in winter and produces a large number of eggs, sometimes as many as 1 million. These are deposited onto stony beds in shallow currents.

It is found almost all over northern Europe to the north of the Balkans and the Pyrenees and in Italy in the watershed of the Po. In England it has become very rare and is possibly extinct. In some places, especially in northern zones, it is an economically important fish, as its meat and liver have a great protein value.

Maximum size and weight: 1 m, 20 kg.
Identifying characteristics: Pelvic fins in front of pectoral pair; anal fin and second dorsal fin very long. One barbel in middle of chin.

1 – adult fish,
2 – detail of head

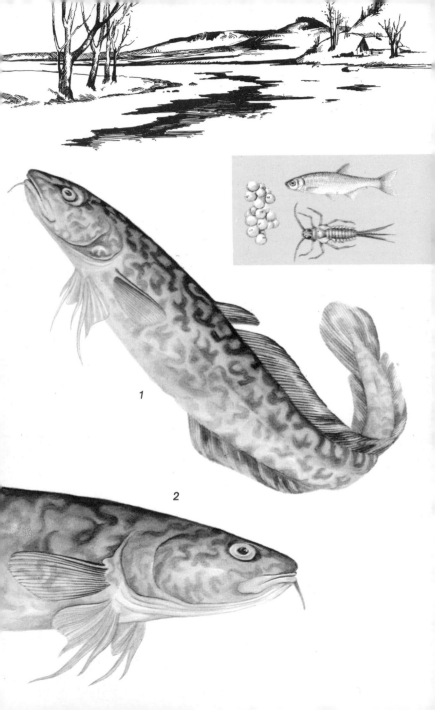

1

2

Flounder

Platichthys flesus

The body of the flounder is very compressed and its height is much greater than its width. It lies on one side and both eyes are located on the same side of its body, usually on the right, sometimes on the left side. The side which is turned away from the bottom and which contains its eyes has a dark pigmentation, whilst the underside is a dull white. Its entire body is covered with very small scales and the lateral line is well developed. The upper part of its body is brownish or olive grey and often has large irregular dark and small brown or yellow spots. The dorsal fin is very long and this and the anal fin are characterized by rows of small spines at their bases, as is the lateral fin. The flounder is a bottom fish and lives gregariously on the sandy bed of shallow, brackish estuary waters close to the river banks, but also far inland upriver. It spawns from January to April in the sea at a depth of 20 to 40 m. Its eggs are planktonic. Small flounders feed largely on small crustaceans, later progressing to worms, molluscs and insect larvae. When they are 10 to 12 mm long, they swim upriver and stay there for 3 to 4 years before again migrating back to the sea.

The flounder inhabits the European coast from the White Sea as far as the Black Sea. Several geographic races are known. In coastal areas it has great commercial value.

A similar species, the starry flounder (*P. stellatus*), lives in the North Pacific and is found in estuaries and rivers on the west coast of America.

Maximum size and weight: 50 cm, 4 kg. *Identifying characteristics:* Body strongly compressed at sides; both eyes located on the right side. Long dorsal fin starts above the eye. Sharp spines present at dorsal and anal fin bases.

1 – adult fish (side view), 2 – view from above (reversed specimen)

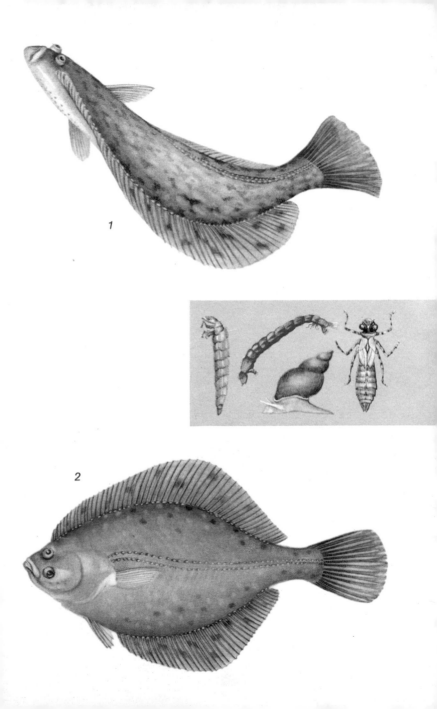

INDUSTRIAL FISHING

Catching fish from the pond is a relatively easy pursuit and pond breeders usually are sufficiently equipped with just one large net, called a dragnet. However, the same process in open waters proves much more difficult, and a number of types of net need to be employed. In recent decades in small rivers, especially in trout waters, the electric fish stunner has proved invaluable in catching trout for artificial breeding. Short, sharp electric shocks stun the fish for several moments, so that it is very easy to catch them without damaging them in any way and then after spawning the fish breeder can release them once again into open water.

The most frequently employed net in rivers, dams and lakes is the seine, which is a long dragnet. This is a very large net, which is often several hundred metres long and ten or more metres high. Rowing boats or motor boats are used to drag the net far out from the bank and spread it in a large semicircle on the water surface. Then the fishermen head quickly back towards the bank with the net floating on the water surface and hanging down into the depths. As soon as the whole length of the bottom cord of the net, which is weighted with lead, is resting on the water bed, the fish have little chance to escape. However, the mesh of the seine net is relatively large, so that it only catches older and larger fish, whilst smaller specimens can easily swim through it and stay in the reservoir.

Also very effective in open waters are gill-nets. The older types of these nets, which consisted of netting of different-sized mesh, have in recent years been replaced by very effective single mesh nets made of thin nylon, which is very firm and can hardly be seen by the fish. Fish which swim into them are caught by the gills or the front half of their body. Gill-nets are usually thirty to forty metres long and three to four metres high. The size of the holes in the net differs according to the size

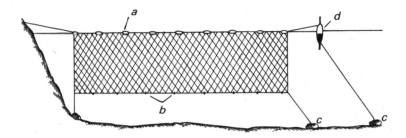

Fig. 8. A set gil-net: a) floats, b) lead weights on the bottom line, c) stone weights, d) buoy.

of the fish which is being caught; a usual size is between 3×3 cm to 12×12 cm and for catching especially large fish 15×15 cm. Gill-nets have floats at the top and weights at the bottom, so that they hang in the water like a curtain. They are normally attached by long cords to a bank or a firmly anchored buoy.

Characteristic of freshwater fisheries are many types of fish traps. Wicker and wire fish-pots and spears are used to catch eel, while systems of stages, leaders and net traps can be employed to catch many other fish species. These nets form a system of funnel-shaped entrances, which are connected

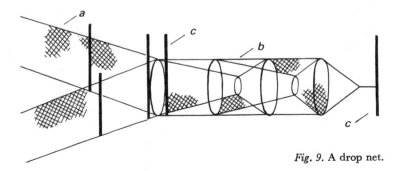

Fig. 9. A drop net.

177

Fig. 10. A fish trap: a) wings,   b) trapping device,   c) stakes.

together by long net leaders. They are set in the shallow parts of rivers, lakes and reservoirs in such a way that the net leaders direct the shoals of fish in search of food into the trap itself.

The catching of fish in dipnets, square-shaped nets fastened at the corners to diagonal crosspieces with flexible rods, has a local importance especially in some larger rivers. The fisherman lifts the net, which is attached to a long pole, every now and then out of the water and in this way catches the fish which otherwise rest on the water bed. This fishing method is especially effective when fish begin to migrate.

The cast net is a cone-shaped one with small, dense holes, which, when thrown, spreads out over the water surface to form a circle. Its perimeter is equipped with weights so that it drops very quickly to the bottom. After this has been accomplished, the fishermen, with the help of fine cords attached to many places along its edges and threaded through the centre, close it up and then the net with its haul of fish is pulled towards the bank. Again in lakes and reservoirs a permanent trapping device is often employed, resembling a sort of a maze, which terminates in traps. However, the latest means of catching fish in large lakes is the electric trawl, which is a large net pulled by one or two boats and equipped with an electric device, which stuns the fish that approach it.

Whilst net fishing is an important branch of industry in both sea and freshwaters and often involves much hard labour, angling is an opportunity for recreation and has millions of followers all over the world. It is one of the most effective methods of relaxing and provides anglers with many pleasant experiences, much excitement and unforgettable adventures. At the same time such sporting fishermen often pay nature back in full for the pleasures it has given them. They are an important aid in the struggle to maintain clean waters and in the protection of nature and the human environment in general.

BIBLIOGRAPHY

Frank, S.: *The Pictorial Encyclopedia of Fishes.* Hamlyn, London, 1971.

Greenwood, P. H. (revisor) & Norman, J. R.: *A History of Fishes.* E. Benn, London, 1975.

Herald, E. S.: *Living Fishes of the World.* Hamish Hamilton, London, 1961.

Holčík, J. & Mihálik, J.: *Freshwater Fishes.* Spring Books, Feltham, Middx, 1968.

Marshall, N. B.: *The Life of Fishes.* Weidenfeld & Nicolson, London, 1965.

McPhail, J. D. & Lindsey, C. C.: *Freshwater Fishes of Northwestern Canada and Alaska.* Fisheries Research Board of Canada, Ottawa, 1970.

Muus, B. J. & Dahlstrom, P.: *The Freshwater Fishes of Britain and Europe.* Collins, London, 1971.

Scott, W. B. & Crossman, E. J.: *Freshwater Fishes of Canada.* Fisheries Research Board of Canada, Ottawa, 1973.

Sterba, G.: *Freshwater Fishes of the World.* Studio Vista, London, 1966.

Wheeler, A.: *The Fishes of the British Isles and North West Europe.* Macmillan, London, 1969.

INDEX OF COMMON NAMES

Asp   106

Barbel   114
—, Southern   114
Bass, Large-mouth Black   166
Bitterling   94
Bleak   116
Bream, Common   120
—, Danube   122
—, Silver   118
Bullhead   164
—, Alpine   164
—, Brown   148
Burbot   172

Carp   132, 134, 136, 138
—, Crucian   128
—, Gibel   130
—, Grass   140
—, Silver   140
Catfish, European   146
Charr   74
Chub   98

Dace   96

Eel, European   150

Flounder   174

Goby, Mottled Black Sea   88
Goldfish, The   130
Grayling   84
Gudgeon   112
—, Danube   112

Houting   82
—, Freshwater   80
Huchen   78

Ide   100

Lampern   50
Lamprey, Brook   52
—, Danube   52
—, Sea   48
Loach, Spined   144
—, Stone   142

Miller's Thumb   164
Minnow   102
Moderlieschen   94
Mud-minnow   88
Mullet, Common Grey   152
—, Golden Grey   152

Nase   110

Orfe   100

Perch   154
Pike   86
Pikeperch   156
—, Eastern   158
Pope   160
Pumpkinseed   168

Roach   90
—, Black Sea   92
—, Danube   92
Rudd   104

Ruffe   160

Salmon   60, 62
Schneider   116
Schraetzer   160
Shad, Allis   58
—, Twaite   58
Smelt   82
Souffie   96
Sterlet   56
Stickleback, Three-spined   170
Streber   162
Sturgeon   54

Tench   108
Trout, Brook   76

—, Brown   68, 70
—, Lake   66
—, Rainbow   72
—, Sea   64

Vendace   80

Weatherfish   142
Wels   146

Zahrte   124
Zander   156
—, Eastern   158
Ziege   126
Zingel   162
Zope   122

INDEX OF LATIN NAMES

Abramis ballerus   122
Abramis brama   120
Abramis sapa   122
Acipenser ruthenus   56
Acipenser sturio   54
Alburnoides bipunctatus   116
Alburnus alburnus   116
Alosa alosa   58
Alosa fallax   58
Anguilla anguilla   150
Aspius aspius   106

Barbus barbus   114
Barbus meridionalis   114
Blicca bjoerkna   118

Carassius auratus gibelio   130
Carassius carassius   128
Chondrostoma nasus   110
Cobitis taenia   144
Coregonus albula   80
Coregonus lavaretus maraena   80
Coregonus oxyrinchus   82
Cottus gobio   164
Cottus poecilopus   164
Ctenopharyngodon idella   140
Cyprinus carpio   132, 134, 136, 138

Esox lucius   86
Eudontomyzon danfordi   52

Gasterosteus aculeatus   170
Gobio gobio   112
Gobio uranoscopus   112

Gymnocephalus cernua   160
Gymnocephalus schraetser   160

Hucho hucho   78
Hypophthalmichthys molitrix   140

Ictalurus nebulosus   148

Lampetra fluviatilis   50
Lampetra planeri   52
Lepomis gibbosus   168
Leucaspius delineatus   94
Leuciscus cephalus   98
Leuciscus idus   100
Leuciscus leuciscus   96
Leuciscus souffia   96
Liza aurata   152
Lota lota   172

Micropterus salmoides   166
Misgurnus fossilis   142
Mugil cephalus   152

Noemacheilus barbatulus   142

Osmerus eperlanus   82

Pelecus cultratus   126
Perca fluviatilis   154
Petromyzon marinus   48
Phoxinus phoxinus   102
Platichthys flesus   174
Proterorhinus marmoratus   88

Rhodeus sericeus amarus   94

Rutilus frisii meidingeri 92
Rutilus pigus 92
Rutilus rutilus 90

Sabanajewia aurata 144
Salmo gairdneri 72
Salmo salar 60, 62
Salmo trutta 64, 66, 68, 70
Salvelinus alpinus 74
Salvelinus fontinalis 76
Scardinius erythrophthalmus 104
Silurus glanis 146

Stizostedion lucioperca 156
Stizostedion volgense 158

Thymallus thymallus 84
Tinca tinca 108

Umbra krameri 88

Vimba vimba 124

Zingel streber 162
Zingel zingel 162